HELP WANTED

moms raising daughters

DARLENE BROCK

the Grit&

D1158941

Help Wanted: Moms Raising Daughters

Published in the U.S. by:
The Grit and Grace Project, P.O. Box 247, Estero, FL 33929
www.thegritandgraceproject.com

Published in association with:
OakTara Publishers
P.O. Box 8, Waterford, VA 20197
www.oaktara.com

Cover design by Yvonne Parks at www.pearcreative.ca

Cover images © www.shutterstock.com, woman holding whiteboard/nakamasa

The Grit & Grace Project logos by Kevin Owen, Owen Studio of SW Fl, Inc.

Author photo © 2011 by Nick Adams Photography.com

Edited by Ramona Cramer Tucker

ISBN: 978-1-60290-280-0

Printed in the USA.

Contents

WANTED

*Seeking women willing to take on
the most difficult job in the world:*
Raising Daughters....

No Experience Necessary

| Job Description |

No experience necessary...?

"HELP WANTED!" was the desperate cry of my heart when I learned I was beginning a new job—one of the most important jobs I'd ever had or will have—and it arrived without a classified ad or notice on a message board. I found myself facing a position I hadn't applied for, didn't possess the required knowledge for, nor had I received the training needed to pull such a complicated job off.

I was beginning a new long-term venture...one I faced with a fearful heart, believing I could easily fail. After all, I was unqualified, lacking any understanding of what would be required to succeed at this new vocation. And I had made absolutely no plan or preparations to even take on, let alone master, this new job. I was blindsided.

My journey began with, of all things, an auto accident. I'd love to tell you that automobile accidents are entirely foreign to me. (It certainly seems an incredibly foolhardy move to reveal one's personal failings on a first meeting, doesn't it? But if I skipped that part of the story it would be a lie.) So I have to admit that these events held a prominent place in my teenage years. By the day of this incident I was an old hand at the necessary actions taken when fenders are crushed. I had the procedure down.

Fortunately for me, this particular accident was not my fault; my car was the one hit from behind. While this fact provided a bit of emotional relief, the accident still was an unbelievable inconvenience. You see, I was on my way to the airport with my husband's college buddy. He'd been visiting us for several days and now needed to fly home. This visit was the first time he and I had met, and up until this moment I don't think I had come off as a complete idiot. (At least I hoped not.) But this was indeed early in our marriage, and I really cared that I looked like the "you done good!" wife, not the "what were you thinking?" woman in the eyes of this college buddy. It certainly wasn't in my plans to blow a good impression in the last thirty minutes.

As this normal day changed quickly, I had to get all the accident stuff out of the way first before we could head for the airport. I managed the process with minor humiliation, and then, purely by the skin of my teeth, we arrived at the terminal just in time. After the drop-off, I headed home exhausted. *The accident must really have whopped me,* I thought, so I took the rest of the day off. I reflected on my other previous accidents.

When I was seventeen, I ran my car into a swamp (yes, real water with green stuff on the top, swamp). Stepping out of the vehicle into waist-deep water, I recovered rather quickly, even though my car didn't. It ran, but the swamp smell was a permanent part of my car ownership. My father said helpfully that the aroma was there to make sure I never forgot where my car had landed.

Then there was the time I pulled out in front of the local state senator's enormous Lincoln Continental. Of course, it didn't receive a scratch, and I felt fine afterwards. It was my Ford Galaxy passenger door that felt all the pain. It never opened easily after that event.

When I was nineteen, I experienced a horrendous front-end collision as I was leaving the parking lot that housed my VW bug while I worked at my first "pay my own rent" job. With a crunched front end and a broken steering wheel from my head's impact, I was quickly placed into an ambulance and driven to the closest hospital. There I received thirteen stitches and a ticket from the delightfully thoughtful, absolutely in the right police officer.

For the life of me, I couldn't understand why my physical response to this accident on the way to the airport was so different. I was older, yes, but not much—only in my late twenties. This hadn't been my worst auto accident; the damage was minor. Determined to look for answers elsewhere, I made an inventory of my symptoms, studying all health diseases that fit any item on my list. I couldn't find a thing.

I wasn't dying of some rare disease—at least not one I could identify. Instead I stayed exhausted for the next three weeks and couldn't figure out why.

Flash Forward a Few Weeks...

Sometimes I can be a little slow…more often than not, I'm simply too distracted. Maybe it's the fact that I have the attention span of a three-year-old. But in this instance, I think I didn't want to consider anything past the car accident or some convenient, yet unnamed, disease. It took awhile to face up to the fact that maybe something else was going on, entirely normal but never before experienced…by me, at least.

I looked at my calendar, counted days three times every way that could be counted, hoping for a different result. My search for truth was in the years when a young woman had to see a doctor for confirmation of calendar evidence, so I called my gynecologist to make the appointment.

Several blurry days later, I arrived at my doctor's doorstep and was quickly escorted to the exam room. When asked, I numbly managed to tell the nurse I needed to ask the doctor something. No other words seemed capable of crossing my lips. My heart was pounding so hard that I was lucky to have conveyed that much.

It wasn't long before the doctor entered the room, kindly asking why I was there. My barely intelligible response? "I guess I need to know if I need to know something." While making a vague calendar reference, I kept my eyes steadfastly on the floor.

That shrewd doctor was somehow able to interpret my inept speech. He graciously smiled, took a pregnancy test, and came back beaming with the delightful news: I was going to have a baby.

I, on the other hand, provided him with an extraordinarily insincere smile. Frozen in place on the exam table, I received my instructions in a completely out-of-body experience while pretending I was ecstatic with his announcement. However, the moment he finished his doctor duties, I ran out the examining room door, past the reception area, and hightailed it out of the office into the parking lot.

When I got into the driver's seat of my car, I burst into tears...and didn't stop crying for a month. (Really, I cried for a whole month! Some of you understand.) I was terrified. I had just managed to understand who I was. I was successful at work, doing a good job building our businesses with my husband, happily married, and feeling pretty good about life in general. But now I had a new job, one in which I was completely without experience and vastly underqualified.

I was a mother. I needed job training, and I needed it fast.

One day I want to be a mother, I thought, *but now?* The timing didn't seem right. Then another thought hit that scared me even more: *I will be responsible for another human being!* Panic was my immediate emotion, and it returned at various times in the years that followed.

I was a mother.
I needed job training,
and I needed it fast.

I knew the instant I heard the news that I didn't have a clue about what made a mother good at her job. Sure, I had been in the workplace since I was seventeen and accomplished things I never thought I could do. But this job seemed over my head. Worse, if I didn't get this one right, I wasn't the only human who would suffer.

Taking a deep breath, I gave myself a lecture. If I could pull off every other endeavor when I was entirely clueless, there had to be a way to do this one as well. I had seen other mothers do it—sometimes very well and other times not so great. To have the best chance of success in this new vocation, I needed to find the good mothers quickly so I could learn from them.

After all, it was a policy of mine, with every new venture I took on, to find others who had done it well before me. The best way to do something well was to emulate those who already had.

The Super Bowl of Mothering

In this case, I needed to unearth those women who had done this job with some degree of success. What better place to look for the best-of-all mom duties than the mothers of Presidents of the United States? These women had to be the Super Bowl of Mothering, I figured.

Through intense research, I discovered amazing stories about these women and stumbled across some great role models who gave this new mom hope.

Sara Delano Roosevelt

Did you know that Franklin Delano Roosevelt was reared by Sara Delano Roosevelt in a New England family of wealth and aristocracy? Franklin was well traveled and educated in the best private schools, even receiving a law degree from Harvard. This family lived with virtually no financial want. Yet when young Franklin was ill in the Groton School Infirmary with scarlet fever, his mother returned from Europe to care for him.

In those days, scarlet fever was highly contagious. All patients were held in quarantine, and only healthcare workers were allowed in the room. Undaunted, this resourceful mother dragged a workman's ladder to the second-story window of her son's room. Each day Sara climbed that ladder and tapped on the window. When it was opened, she talked to and read to her son, caring for him in the only way she could.

> *This resourceful mother dragged a*
> *workman's ladder to the second-story window*
> *of her son's room.*

The refinement, dignity, and wealth of this world-traveled woman couldn't compete with the nature of motherhood to keep her off that ladder. She was there performing her job when her son needed her most.

Dorothy Gardner King

In the year 1913, under the cover of darkness, Dorothy Gardner King boarded a taxi with her sixteen-day-old son in her arms. They were fleeing from an abusive husband and father. Dorothy had grown up in a prominent family and married into affluence. In those days a woman simply didn't leave a husband of position, especially with child in hand. A divorce required that each act of violence be publicly detailed and witnessed, bringing unwanted scrutiny upon prominent families. Yet Dorothy courageously did just that. She rescued her child from a life of violence, filed for divorce, and left an abusive household behind.

Nearly three years later Dorothy Gardner King married a

common paint salesman who had only an eighth-grade education. A delightful, loving man, Jerry Ford became the instant father of a three-year-old son. He promptly gave his full name to this child, Gerald Rudolph Ford, raising the boy as his own. The reward of Dorothy's unselfish act of protection was seen in the life of the 38th President of the United States.

Martha Young Truman

Harry Truman was reared on farmland in Kansas. Living in Middle America, Harry's mother, Martha Young Truman, taught hard work, as well as personal innovation and culture. This middle-class family worked the land together, awakening at 4:00 a.m. to complete the farm chores.

But Martha Truman, mother to this future president, made sure her son was armed with the tools and dreams to achieve his destiny. Living within the budget of managing a farm, Martha scraped together the needed funds to purchase an expensive set of books entitled *Great Men and Famous Women*. Harry's education consisted of twelve years at public school, graduating with a high school diploma; he never attended one day of college. These works, given to him by his mother, fueled the inspiration of this young farmer's son. Because Martha recognized Truman's voracious appetite for knowledge through the written word, she sacrificed to provide the education he needed to achieve greatness.

A Doable Job?

The more I read about these women, the more I liked them. They figured out their mothering along the way, and that gave me hope. If these women in their varied roles, vastly different financial status, and unique personalities could raise a President, my own mother job appeared doable. These were truly "ordinary" women who performed mothering tasks extra-ordinarily well. Other than the time in which they lived, they weren't different than we mothers today. They didn't know what their sons would become; they merely set out to accomplish their motherhood profession and face the challenges before them.

After a month, when the crying finally dried up, I began to believe I could do the mothering thing...at least if the baby was a boy. I could handle one of those. The President moms had boys, and I had worked with recording-artist bands entirely comprised of boys, so getting along with the male gender was a piece of cake for me.

With that relief, my mind cleared. I felt good about being pregnant and began planning a life with sons. Boys spit, scratched, romped, stood on their heads in the middle of class (or when you were in the middle of a sentence, attempting to talk with them), caught bugs, and stayed perpetually dirty. When they got mad, it happened quickly but was soon forgotten. With boys, there were no grudges, no simmering attitudes or jealousy, no hidden complexities. I knew everything would work out fine. What had I worried about anyway? I told myself.

But life was not as predictable as I'd thought. My surprise? I would become the mother of two *girls*.

I was certain any girl entrusted to my care would suffer merely because she was mine...and I was ill prepared for the challenges that are uniquely feminine.

Life was not as predictable as I'd thought.

Every female understands our gender can and will be led by emotion. We laugh louder, cry more easily, and have higher highs and lower lows than our male counterparts. We find ourselves passionate for a good cause and equally passionate when the cause is not so good. In anger, females attack with the amazing power of words. We can hold on to an injustice; our memories are long and often unforgiving. We are clever and powerful, simply because we are women. We are masters of manipulation, whether with a smile or silence, leaving the male population intensely puzzled. Indeed, women are the more challenging, complex gender. So with this perspective, I was certain my daughters could outwit, out-strategize, and overall emotionally wear me out.

Looking back now, I thank God that he thought differently than I did and that he understands far more about human nature than I ever could with my simple, foolish evaluations. He blessed me. Yes, *blessed me* with girls. It was no accident. The first was born seven months after my doctor visit; the next was birthed four years after that. My daughters *are* complex, no doubt. But they are also delightful, loving, giving, endearing, nurturing, and, most days, a real joy. They dance into a room...and into my heart.

I was destined to rear two females in the fast-paced, challenging, information age we live in. They would be growing up with multiple, conflicting definitions of who they should be as girls, and then as women. These ideas would not only come from me, as their mother, by watching my actions and hearing my words, but also from television, film, education, music, video games, and Barbie dolls. Other women in our culture, from their platforms as entertainers, businesswomen, teachers, etc., would be determined to help me train my girls (whether I wanted them to or not). Fear struck one more time as I realized there were many things I didn't want my girls to be taught.

So I dug in even deeper to explore this multifaceted role of motherhood.

It was then I realized this motherhood thing is not merely one job. Mothers are not just "Mom." They fulfill a variety of positions and responsibilities. We are required to be professor, counselor, bodyguard, and coach; we must brainstorm, create, figure out, simplify, organize, protect, and encourage. And like many of you, I had to do all of this while fulfilling another job outside the home.

9

So, armed with what information I could gather, I set out to achieve my objective: raising productive, successful, healthy, and whole young ladies.

This book is about what I learned—about the jobs you need to master, the advice from other women that helped me, as well as some realities about the life and culture we live in that informed my perspective. You will experience both success and failure. But I'm living proof to tell you: Mom, your goal can be accomplished, and accomplished well! I know it every time I interact with my now grown daughters, Loren and Chelsea, and see the ways in which they are making a difference in their own fields of film making and teaching.

You *can* take on the most difficult job in the world—raising daughters—and not only live to tell about it, but smile along the way too.

HELP WANTED!

Seeking women willing to take
the most difficult job in the world…

(No experience necessary)

- Coach
- Creative Counselor
- Time Manager
- Media Director
- Academic Advocate
- Professor of Gender Studies
- Relationship Counselor
- Sex Ed Teacher
- Financial Consultant
- Bodyguard
- Communications Specialist
- In-home Demonstrator
- Military Strategist

1

Wanted
Coach

| Job Description |

Teach player techniques, rules, strategies, and tactics. Condition athlete for activities, strength, and endurance. Instruct player in sportsmanship, cooperation, work ethic, and responsibility. Monitor conduct of player and respond to injuries.

C*oaching?* you're saying. *What does that have to do with rearing daughters?*

Everything. This is truly the first position a mother has to accept: becoming the Coach. If you're not an athlete, not to worry. I'm not, either. Playing sports truly wasn't and isn't my thing. I had many other interests, including art and music. But this job doesn't have a thing to do with athletic ability. You can be what is called in our home "a girlie girl" and still get this one right.

Immediately following the manual-labor tasks of motherhood, coaching begins. At the end of the early days, you know the blur where you believe sleep will never again be part of your life. Every few hours you feed, change diapers, burp, wash, change diapers, feed, burp, pick up, rock, feed, burp, clean up, change diapers, give a bath, and rock again...all the while begging God to give you both that much-needed rest. It's when the sleep finally returns and these manual-labor tasks become automatic, you become the Coach. The effective performance of this position will, without a doubt, determine the success of every other job for the next eighteen years.

A Coach is the leader, the authority, the person responsible for the accomplishments of the players.

A Coach has to draw on experience and be confident in creating the plays—also a must for mothering daughters.

A Coach sets the team rules and consequences for inappropriate conduct; so does a mother.

A Coach is the leader, the authority, the person responsible for the accomplishments of the players.

A Coach responds to injuries; well, I can tell you firsthand there's a boatload of those in mothering daughters.

A Coach motivates and inspires—a crucial duty of mothers.

And a Coach is aware that each player is an independent decision-maker. If the players have a good coach who leads them well, their good decisions become much easier and their bad decisions less desirable.

Friend—or Mom?

A recent study revealed that 43 percent of today's parents are seeking acceptance and friendship from their teens,. Forty percent of these parents surveyed said they would buy their children everything they wanted to accomplish their primary objective: to be their child's best friend. In theory this sounds like a good plan. Who doesn't want their child to like them? to share private thoughts as a friend would? to hang out? to have deep meaningful conversations and friendly fun?

But there's an unintended byproduct to this desire: in order to maintain a position of friendship one must abdicate a position of authority. Friends are generally not instructional. Friendship does not discipline, set rules, protect, give insight, and seldom challenges incorrect acts. Parenting does. Friends don't generally inspire and motivate you to become more in life. Parents do. By desiring to be a member of the friendship club these parents are missing a significant reality. A child will have many friends, but as parents, we're it.

Whether you are a birth parent, a foster parent, an adoptive parent, or a stepparent, the privileged role you play in your daughter's life is exclusive. You are not part of the team; you are the Coach. You are singularly the most influential person in your daughter's life.

I can't stress enough how important this job is. No one can replace your role and make an impact on your girl the way you can. This relationship is vital. Without it, the effects on your daughter will be immense and will last forever. Does this bring fear? Indeed it should. But don't let that thought paralyze you. Motherhood is a manageable task if you stay the course. And just wait—at times it'll even be inspiring when you, as the Coach, see your daughter make that winning play.

> *You are singularly*
> *the most influential person*
> *in your daughter's life.*

For all of you mothers, like myself, who experienced days (or months or years) of relational panic with your daughters, I have a wonderful piece of "after the fact" knowledge to give you hope. There will be times you will wonder if your daughter will ever become your friend if you're an effective Coach. You'll watch that daughter storm off toward her room and desperately wonder, *Will she hate me forever? Am I always going to be the one who just doesn't understand?*

Real-life experience with both my daughters taught me that neither of those fears is real. If you're committed to be a great mom and you maintain the position of Coach that your daughter needs (whether she wants to admit it or not), you'll become her friend. And the relationship formed will be a much deeper, more meaningful one than she'll have with her peers. The kind of relationship transcending time, distance, and life obstacles. A relationship that runs so strong your heart will thrill with what you and your daughter mean to each other.

The mother who performs her duties from a fearful, pacifying place, always trying to be her daughter's friend, will never have the privilege of experiencing this profound relationship because the daughter will never develop a healthy respect for her mother. But the mother who holds firm to the position of Coach? She'll experience lifelong benefits!

Experience Is a Great Teacher

It takes strength, determination, and courage to maintain this leadership role—a strength that comes from confidence in your abilities, talents, and knowledge you have garnered in life. This is the time when you, the mother, must evaluate who *you* are, aside from your roles, and believe you are capable to undertake whatever you decide to pursue.

Most coaches were, at one time, players. How do they begin their jobs as coaches, then? They call upon the experience they gained by simply performing the tasks on the field or in the court wherever their sport led them. This is no different for mothers. Begin by drawing upon your experience. You were once a girl, dealing with bad hair days, the challenge of multiplication tables, boyfriend struggles, and the vicious putdowns of mean girls (that is, unless *you* were the mean girl. But since then, you've learned a few things, haven't you?) Life has taught you what you need to know to relate to what your daughter is experiencing right now and along the way. And you can use that knowledge to both of your benefit even when you get the "you don't understand, Mom. That was a million years ago" line.

Coaches also watch a lot of tapes. You know, the ones that show how the other team makes their plays, what their mistakes are, and areas where they are weak. In addition to watching other players Coaches closely watch how their own team is performing. This is relevant to you, Mom. You or someone you know has made a multitude of life decisions and actions that led to specific consequences:

- Driving too fast can wreck a car.
- Run out in the street, you get hit.
- Put a kernel of corn in your nose, and it can get stuck.
- The way to get pregnant is to have sex.
- Touch a hot pot, you get burned.

You've seen these consequences; perhaps you've lived them yourself. They aren't rocket science. So add all of these "truth and consequences" statements to your information base and set the rules, determine the plays.

Use your strengths

Think about what you have accomplished in your previous "career." What classes in school did you excel in? In what jobs have you performed the best? Which of your talents accomplished success in your past? Are you a good organizer? Do you inspire others to success? Are you creative, logical, or mathematical? The duties you perform, as a mother will draw upon the same abilities as those you have already used.

Take time now to write your list of strengths and then ponder them. They'll be just what you need for this motherhood job, as well as using the information you have collected while living your life.

My List of Strengths

- _____

- _____

- _____

- _____

- _____

- _____

- _____

- _____

No coaches are identical in their abilities, and neither are mothers. Your unique mothering style—your strengths, talents, and the way you live your life will be a perfect match for your daughter. So instead of trying to be like everyone else, why not be exactly who your daughter needs? You! It doesn't matter if your daughter entered your life through childbirth, adoption, or marriage, YOU ARE IT—THE ONE AND ONLY! You can, and you will, do your job well.

*Instead of trying to
be like everyone else,
why not be exactly who
your daughter needs? You!*

But that doesn't mean they won't be days where you'll be thinking, *I don't have a clue what to do. I'm out of control, my daughter's out of control, and I just want to stop this world and get off.* Like fighters going to their respective corners, you'll need to send your daughter to her room and you'll need to go to yours so you can both calm down and think rationally. At such times, when you know you're over your head, take a step back. Remind yourself that this job can and will be accomplished by you. Then leave your corner with a clear mind and a confident heart and begin again.

As difficult and daunting as this work can seem, I can assure you it's amazingly simple. Simple rules, simple plays, simple consequences—as they say in team sports, "back to the fundamentals." In our multitude of theories, books, and philosophies regarding motherhood, it's easy to lose track of the simple. I believe the mothers before us understood this principle far better than we do today. That's why we can learn so much from them.

Gutsy Grandma Bunger

I was six years old, playing in the living room of my great grandmother's home, one of my favorite places in the entire world to be. That's because Grandma Bunger was a special lady. Four-foot-eleven, mother of twelve, she had some of the best costume jewelry, hats, and gloves ever seen by a little girl. On each visit she would let us cousins raid her closet and parade down the stairs, tripping over too-big shoes, with hats falling into our eyes, and our arms so heavily bejeweled we could hardly hold them up.

We were the cousins, fourth generation. We landed on our grandmother's doorstep like an army invading the Promise Land. Having twelve children of her own, Grandma Bunger had a plethora of grandchildren, which were our parents, and even more great grandchildren. I couldn't count how many of us there were. All I knew then was we had fun.

We spent our days together dressing in her clothes, going through her junk drawers, which held wonderful treasures, and eating our meals in every corner of the house. The parents and grandparents would talk, argue, laugh, and cry together. The smells from the kitchen would be sweet.

This day was no different than most, the family was busy visiting, mostly talking over each other as they often did, and laughter was abundant. Suddenly a huge commotion arose in the kitchen. I heard the voices of Grandma, Aunt Juanita, and Uncle Jack, and it didn't sound good.

Then the clamor headed my direction—from the kitchen, through the dining room, into the living room, and right out the front door. Grandma was chasing Uncle Jack, a six-foot, more than two-hundred-pound man, through the house and out the front door, hitting him with her broom. You see, he had come home drunk, and when drunk, he could get mean. He had hit Aunt Juanita, and Grandma would not have any of this.

She knew the fundamentals.
To her, life was simple.

So as a young girl, I watched as Uncle Jack ran for his life. He was no match for this lady. Grandma, less than half his size, meant business and we all knew it. She knew the fundamentals. To her, life was simple. This was unacceptable conduct that she would not allow, no matter how big the challenge.

Grandma Bunger was my hero.

But lest you think she was perfect, so you can't relate to her, let me tell you a little more about this grand lady. Ethel Anna Berry was born July 1, 1881 in a small town in Indiana. She didn't live a flawless life; she had a fair amount of heartache. In May 1899 my not-married grandmother bore a son. I can only imagine the plight of an eighteen-year-old, single and pregnant before the turn of the twentieth century.

Two years later she married my great grandfather, a man who never accepted her out-of-wedlock child since he was not the father. Together they had another eleven children. Sadly, she outlived several of her own children: two died as infants, one in a war, and another from cancer.

Grandma Bunger indeed had a tough life with an abundance of trials and struggles. Yet the woman I knew was kind and loving, smiling often, as she stood as the pillar of a very large family. She worked hard through the week, sewing the family clothes, gardening and cooking, performing household duties on machines and in ways we can't begin to understand with today's technology. She had a full-time job with these duties in addition to raising her children. Sunday morning found her with gloves and hat on, dressed in her Sunday best for the weekly church service.

Grandma Bunger was strong: she knew exactly who she was, what she believed, how she wanted to live, and what she wanted for her family. Although she had personal shortcomings—as all of us do—she predetermined which goals she wanted to achieve and stuck with the basics. She knew the fundamentals, backwards and forwards. We as mothers can pursue the same thing—with the same success!

Acting As Coach

A Coach assembles a team, seeking members with abilities to help win a championship. They believe in those players, know their potential, and will take whatever action is necessary to ensure that players maintain the conduct required to reach the goal. A mother is no different, except for one area: we don't draft our daughters to join the team. They are either birthed to us, we receive them through adoption or perhaps you become a stepmother by marriage. (Some days you might wish there had been a daughter draft and perhaps you could have chosen the less-argumentative version....but it just doesn't work that way.)

Bench 'em!

The one thing we must do is take action to maintain conduct. We have to be willing to bench them. When necessary, we have no choice but to discipline. This knowledge I gained by real-life exhausting experience.

I'm a coffee drinker, the kind who has to have two cups of incredibly strong coffee in the morning to carry on an even somewhat intelligent conversation. Prior to that dose of caffeine I stare and stumble to the kitchen, grumbling the entire way. My family knows to stay clear, and my husband has my first cup of coffee made and waiting on the counter for the moment I arrive.

When Loren, my first child, turned two, she was unaware and uncaring of this inadequacy of her mother. She was out of bed every morning and ready to hit the ground running. But with this willful child, the first act was almost daily one of defiance. I contend that those who believe humans are inherently good have never had a willful two-year old. There is no stronger evidence of sin nature in humanity than the two-year-old who is defiant for no other reason than they simply want to be.

I contend that those
who believe humans are inherently good have
never had a willful two-year old.

Our mornings would begin much too early with repeated calls of "Mommy" emanating from her bedroom. I would finally appear at the door to her room and stumble in to get Loren out of bed. The constant source of noise in our home, Loren chattered from the moment she awakened. I would hug her, kiss her, and carry her to the living room, setting her in front of the television to watch *Sesame Street.* Then off I'd go for that first life-saving cup of coffee.

From the time I left her watching Big Bird to the moment I returned with coffee in hand was never more than two minutes. The kitchen was only a few feet away, and all I had to do was pour (thanks again to my husband). However, it still amazes me that, in that brief amount of time, I couldn't complete even that simple task without my daughter challenging some level of authority. And the repertoire of her willful acts was huge.

Even though she was armed with the knowledge that the dog's tail was not to be pulled, I would find her chasing him with a vengeance, leaping upon him with tail firmly in hand. Or she would walk quietly from her seated position to the bookshelf on the other side of the room. From the kitchen I would hear book after book tossed onto the floor. Sometimes my return from the kitchen would not find her in the den but in the bathroom, dunking her toys into the toilet with glee. It was when I encountered this willful child that I gritted my teeth, steeled my will, and set to work.

You see, I was the Coach, and this was my job. When my daughter defied the rules, I had to enforce them. I must say, these weren't some of my great and valiant life moments; they were born of necessity. I was not brave. In fact, some days I helplessly looked around the room for anyone else willing to fill this role. When I would plead "At least let me drink my first cup of coffee," Loren would stare me straight in the eye and run headlong to fulfill her mission. That two-year-old was smart. She was challenging my authority at my absolute weakest moment, and she knew it.

There were days in that battle period of my job that I was ready to throw in the towel. Every time I thought, *I'm too tired today. This one instance won't kill either of us, so I'll just let it go and ignore her,* I'd remind myself, *This same will is going to turn sixteen. She'll date, drive a car, and leave for college. If I don't hold to the rules now, what will she try to do then?*

Envisioning this defiance in a child driving a car and missing curfew struck terror in this mother's bones. I knew I needed to be in charge while she was still shorter than me. To succeed in the task of motherhood, I couldn't shrink from the challenge, no matter how difficult it turned out to be.

I knew I needed to be in charge while she was still shorter than me.

But know this, Mom. If you didn't enforce the rules when your daughter was two, you still can. And you still should. At six or sixteen, it's never too late. Will it be harder? Certainly. Your daughter will also have more verbal responses than a two-year-old would, but the defiance is the same. There are days you'll have to bench your daughter.

How do you do that? The ways to bench change with temperament (hers not yours) age, and offense. Most often the best penalty is the one that matters to them the most: a favorite toy, time on the computer or the phone, a time-out, and, yes, I do believe spanking is sometimes appropriate as well depending on the age, the offense, and the recurring nature of the offense.

Why discipline with something your daughter loves? One of my daughters hated time-outs. Not being able to be in the middle of life killed her. My other daughter had a dreamland that resided in her mind; she could visit it while sitting still in time-out and be happy as a lark. So time-out never worked for that child. That's why it's important to pick the discipline appropriately.

Get used to "Monday Morning Quarterbacks"

Has there ever been a coach for any team who is not criticized, challenged, or second-guessed? There's an easy answer to that question: nope, not ever. Even if you are not a follower of sports yourself, you've heard the grumbling from the group in your family room. This is just as true in the role of mother. Your mother, mother-in-law, friends, society, schools, churches, and even your own daughter can become "Monday Morning Quarterbacks." They will feel the need to tell you what you did wrong. So you didn't always call the right play, didn't bench the player when you should have, or you benched the player when you shouldn't have. Well, so what? Take advice from the sources you trust and leave the rest at the door. It doesn't take a perfect coach to be a great coach.

These duties might sound ominous to you. Let me tell you, they're not the most enjoyable tasks. But put them in perspective. When your thirteen-year-old daughter marches up the steps proclaiming, "I'm so mad at you!" your heart probably isn't warmed. Most likely, you're mad at her too and hopefully trying hard not to show it. Then an hour later she returns to rummage for food in the kitchen. (Get used to it: teenagers are always hungry.) She plops down next to you on the couch and proceeds to make a complete cookie-and-cracker mess. All the while she's chattering away, and it hits you: *She still likes me.*

It doesn't take a perfect coach to be a great coach.

Then there are days you feel someone must have gotten this one wrong. Who decided you were capable of being mother to a daughter, especially to this one who has her own unique personality that can make every self-assured bone in your body crumble?

When all of these self-doubts hit, let me assure you: You were made to be the perfect mother for your daughter. The pairing of the two of you is no accident. You are equipped with the talents, abilities, and gifts not only to do this job, but to do it well. Your daughter was given to you and you to your daughter. This is a perfect match.

Then there are the days you realize your inspiration and motivation has paid off. Your daughter has made a good play! The multiplication tables are learned, the mean girl is brushed off, and recovery from heartbreak is achieved.

Trust that on the good days, as well as the hard days, you will find the right words, the right actions, and the right responses to coach your daughter effectively. Concentrate on doing this job first, and the rest of the jobs become a little easier.

2

WANTED
Creative Counselor

| Job Description |

Cultivate a positive climate that will encourage the child's uniqueness, gifts, and creativity. Establish a relationship with the child based upon the counselor's understanding of counselor's and child's creativity and purpose. Create activities that ensure development of all talents and gifts innately within the child.

E ach summer, while I was growing up in Indiana, my mother would help me do a new project. One year we made a dollhouse out of a cardboard box. Another time we redecorated my bedroom—from pink frills to hip paisley wallpaper on, of all places, my ceiling. I learned at a young age how wonderful it is to be creative and embrace originality.

But one particular summer I remember the most—the summer I was learning to sew. Armed with a 1960s Singer Sewing machine, fabric, snaps, thread, straight pins, and scissors I began that year's summer project. My mother was determined to teach me to sew, and what better way to learn but on clothes for my Barbie dolls? I wanted the hippest, most stylish dolls anyone had ever seen, and my mother was going to help me.

So on a Saturday we made a trip to the local fabric store and discovered preprinted fabric, the kind where the skirt and top shape were already printed onto the muslin fabric and all you had to do was cut and sew. We picked out and purchased the only selection they had.

Once back at home I began my quest toward creativity and, from my mother's point of view, my initiation into sewing.

Diligently cutting out the shapes with my mother by my side helping me, I labored over the fabric. No more of this buying Mattel line outfits for me. I was forging a new path. My dolls were going to have special clothes uniquely made for them. I carefully cut and pinned each piece. Placing my foot on the sewing pedal, I often ran it far too fast as I got used to the rhythm. (I'm sure my mother held her breath as I barely missed stitching my finger.) I sewed each and every tiny item on the one-yard piece of fabric. I'm sure there were no more than two or three outfits, but it became my personal mission to finish them all.

After days of cutting, pinning, and sewing, my creations were complete. I was delighted. I had brand-new clothes that *I* had made for my Barbie dolls. None of the neighbor girls had the same ones I did. I was so proud.

That is, at least at first. You see, the problem with preprinted fabric was that it was available to everyone. The only thing any little girl had to do was walk into the fabric store, purchase the same length of fabric we did, and their dolls' outfits would look identical to mine. It didn't take long for my excitement about my creations to diminish. Every Barbie doll would look no different than my own—the very thing I wanted to change.

It became imperative to find something I could do again to set my Barbie dolls apart. This was my mother's and my next pursuit. At the same fabric store we made a new discovery: you could buy patterns to make clothes with fabric of your own choice...even fabric you already had at home. I carefully selected the appropriate patterns for the clothing I wanted to create.

Arriving home with sack in hand, I was anxious to begin. Laying the patterns on the small pieces of cloth left over from dresses my mother had made for me, I pinned them carefully. I was successful in this endeavor, only sticking myself once or twice. A Barbie doll skirt was my first independent creation. It was fairly simple to cut the semicircle pattern, sew it, and put a snap on it, but I felt I had made a great accomplishment. Next was the matching top. This was a little more difficult. The pattern was more intricate, and the cutting had to be more exact. With help from my mother, I accomplished this task too.

This cutting and sewing went on the entire summer. Taking scraps of material left from my mother's sewing projects, I made clothes for my dolls. In fact, I created an entire wardrobe! New dresses, pants, formals, skirts, and tops for my dolls matched my own clothes—all with patterns from the fabric store. I was truly on a roll. Yet, never satisfied, I decided it was time to make my own designs.

Now the real fun began. Out with the patterns, I was going to sew freestyle. I took the scissors and cut what I thought would be an appropriate length for a formal dress. Sewing it together on each side, with ribbon on the neck and fake fur around the hem, I concocted one of the most original Barbie formals ever seen…even if it didn't hang quite right, the seams were a bit off, and the ribbon crooked. Then, to top it off, my mother had enough scraps of fake fur that I could make a coat for my doll to match. A bulky, furry thing when it was done, it probably could have fit two Ken dolls standing side to side. But I was delighted. This was truly a fine outfit! Barbie was ready to go out on the town.

That formal Barbie attire turned out to be only the beginning of my original designs. Of all the things I made that summer, my favorites were the ones made of my own dreams—not using any preexisting pattern, but only what I wanted my creations to be. They were dresses and formals, skirts and accessories that were uniquely mine. They had buttons, rhinestones, and sequins in the strangest places on the most unusual clothes. Yet, to me, my Barbie had never looked finer.

*Of all the things I made that summer,
my favorites were the ones made
of my own dreams.*

Astonished by Originality

Recently, as I was reading the book of Romans, I was abruptly struck by a Scripture that nearly flew off the page. Since my attention span as an adult is still equivalent to a three-year-old's, I occasionally have to be jostled to heed what I really need to hear. The words were ones I'd heard and taken to heart a long time ago, yet suddenly they seemed fresh and alive:

Do not conform any longer to the pattern of this world, but be transformed by the renewing of your mind. Then you will be able to test and approve what God's will is— his good, pleasing and perfect will.
—ROMANS 12:2

As I often do with Scripture, I immediately thought, *What in the world does that* really *mean?* Nonconformity to a pattern, transformation, and then you will find God's will—not only that but his *perfect* will?

In my faith, I base all assumptions upon the fact that I believe in a divine creator. A God who is supreme, original, and enormously smarter than I am. He would have to be to have made this world. Everything he created was indeed freehand—no pattern!—and he apparently has the same expectations of us.

In a quest to discover what is meant by originality, the antithesis of patterns, the most appropriate place to begin is in creation. Have you ever gone to a zoo or an aquarium? In all the creatures there is originality galore! Stay even closer to home and sit in the grass in your back yard or a nearby park. I'm not talking about sitting in a chair but truly *in the grass,* where you are in the middle of the activity. Observe the flowers, bugs, bees, butterflies, rabbits, lizards, blades, leaves, tree branches, bark, sky, clouds, and the wind's effect. Take in the sights, sounds, and smells. Follow the movement and detail around you, the simplicity of the sky, the complexity of the flower petal, and the energy of the bugs and animals.

If you pay attention, you'll be astonished that the color green is a million different shades and hues. There is no end in the creativity right outside your door. Beautiful, original, and harmonious, every corner of creation offers amazement. It has always seemed to take a lot more faith to believe this all "just happened" than to believe in intelligent design. Yet try to define the Designer. Talk about not following a pattern, God set the standard on originality and uniqueness. His innovation through the creation process is reflected in the marvelous world around us, as well as in the intriguing individuals he created. There is not one item in creation that is identical to another.

Take noses, for example. The next time you're in a meeting with a group of people, sneak a peek at each person's nose. (You can get by with this kind of examination since the nose is so near people's eyes; they'll just think you have good eye contact!) After your survey, you'll be surprised by how different they all are—fat, narrow, long, short, with a bump in the middle, at the end, or no bump at all. Talk about creativity, and that's simply a nose!

The Patterns We Conform To

In this creative nature is one of our most important job duties as a mother—that of Creative Counselor. But to understand and effectively counsel on originality or creativity, we have to first understand the *counter* characteristic—sameness or patterns.

The purpose of a pattern is to duplicate something. *Webster's* dictionary defines it as "a form or model proposed for imitation." An item of clothing, a repeated design on wallpaper, a mold for metal piece reproduction, the flight path of an airplane—these are all examples of patterns. To follow a pattern, we continue in the same route again and again—a path that has already been created and traversed. When I consider the Scripture that states we are not to conform to a pattern, I believe we, as mothers, are charged to not reproduce what we see but to be original. And we are tasked to rear originals as well.

A requirement to train our daughters in the avoidance of unoriginality means realizing and pondering the two patterns we find ourselves conforming to.

The normal American route

The first pattern is created by the world we live in and by the paths of people around us. We should never follow others' lives and actions just because they do so and it seems the normal American route.

I still remember my mom saying, "If your friends jumped off a bridge, would you?" As much as I hated that phrase as a teenager, I've said the same thing to my daughters when they were teenagers. The temptation to repeat some things your mother told you is simply irresistible, isn't it? After all, it's fun to watch the rolling eyeballs....

I still remember my mom saying,
"If your friends jumped off a bridge,
would you?"

The first pattern of this world is one that encourages duplication and discourages individuality while at the same time pretending independence. This pattern is designed to destroy your daughter's uniqueness. It will end in the degradation of their self-esteem, and derail them from the purpose they were created for.

It's easy for us to look at the world of music, film, television, the internet, the sexual revolution, and even the clothing industry as having a negative effect on our children. But if we're truly honest, we must also look at soccer teams, the women's movement, ballet class, education, poverty, the American church, and the moors of middle class. Some of the most effective influences over and diversions to the well-being of our girls are subtle. These are wrought while we try to fulfill all the cultural expectations we place upon ourselves. So, Mom, it's time for you to take the bull by the horns. Examine every one of these influences. Dissect them to determine how to control their result. Look around and figure out what unhealthy influences are hitting your daughters. Then decide how best to handle the information from this time forward.

A very real problem with the pattern set before us in America is its hidden sameness. This is teaching young girls a value system—and it's available in nearly every medium (television, movies, magazines, books, etc.)—that's destructive to God's original design for a woman.

My elder daughter was thirteen when she announced she was getting a tattoo.

Here's what I mean. Every mother has at one time or another heard the all-too-familiar phrases that go something like this: "But Jennifer's mom said she could go" or, "It's what all of the girls at school wear." Then here's one of my personal favorites: "All of my friends get to do it...you just don't trust me." Mom, it will take all of your originality and creativity to respond, but you must. Why

33

would you follow a course just because "everybody's doing it"?

My elder daughter was thirteen when she announced she was getting a tattoo. This was the child who was terrified of needles and cried each time we headed to a doctor. I knew she'd never face a needle voluntarily no matter how much she wanted to make me think this was imperative to her life goals. So I happily (on the surface at least) went along with it. I told her tattoos were an important decision, because they were permanent. I said I'd be more than happy to go with her and look over what kind of pictures she might want. We could even go to the library first and see if we could find books on tattoo designs. Indeed this tattoo would be with her for life, so it should be very pretty.

Clearly Loren was disappointed that I didn't take the bait for a fight. At that particular stage of thirteen, she was only interested in irritating me. To show me she was all grown up and independent, she had determined to do something she thought I might not like. But when I didn't react negatively, it was astounding how quickly that conversation was forgotten. Not another word was said about a tattoo ever again.

Now if you're reading this and you have a tattoo, let me be quick to say I'm not making a judgment on tattoos. I've seen some incredibly beautiful ones. Talk about creativity—talented artists have fashioned some of these designs, and they are indeed a work of art. But thirteen years of age was definitely not the time in life to make a decision on something that permanent. A decision like that probably should be made when you're at least thirty. Don't we all change our minds on almost everything after thirty? It's better to wait until you're out of high school to do something that's not easily changed.

But that day when my daughter announced her tattoo, I had a choice. I could respond with the traditional, "Oh no, you're not, young lady. You absolutely will *not* get a tattoo!" or I could face the confrontation with an original approach that gave me a much better chance at success with this willful thirteen-year-old.

And guess what? On that day, success was mine.

You see, originality and creativity really does work. And it gets your daughter's attention, too.

Then there's my younger daughter, Chelsea. She had pink hair in elementary school. Yes, I realize that's a bit different from the norm, and some mothers would be extremely uncomfortable with hair that color, but for Chelsea, it was self- expression. It was only streaks the length of a few strands or the hair ends, but she loved her pink hair. And each time we varied how we put the color in. So when she asked me about it the first time, I said it was fine; we'd make it a mother-daughter project. *How odd,* I thought. *My mom taught me to sew, and I'm coloring my daughter's hair pink to spend time with her.*

My daughter Chelsea had pink hair in elementary school.

So off Chelsea and I went to the artsy downtown store that sold weird temporary hair color and purchased one jar labeled Bright Punky Pink. After dinner, we spent the rest of the evening accomplishing her creation. How we dyed her hair was her choice. It was her style and design, and she was very particular on the execution. Putting on the color-safe gloves and wrapping my daughter completely in old towels, I placed pink hair color in two two-foot lengths of hair on each side of her sweet face.

The next day my eight-year-old attended elementary school with pink streaks. She was extremely delighted with the look. I have no idea what the other mothers thought of either Chelsea or me, and I didn't care to know. What others thought didn't matter. I was focused on what's most important: doing whatever it takes to build a strong mother-daughter relationship. With my girls, I always wanted to allow for originality and creativity.

Many things were important to Loren and Chelsea that really didn't matter to me. They were not life-changing ideas. Early on, I had made a commitment to give my best to my daughters by focusing on the issues that were important in the long-term, not the ones with short-term effects. They could have pink hair if their hearts were compassionate. Unusual and unique clothes didn't scare me if they maintained modesty. Triple-piercing their ears would be in the family budget if they concentrated on their school work and worked to achieve life success.

The art of creative counseling requires a mom to focus on the important issues to help ensure life success.

Your crusade as a mom is for the hearts and souls of your daughters. That's why, short of an indecent wardrobe, clothing doesn't matter, hair color doesn't matter, and even tattoos and piercings don't matter. Those are all short-term things. Yet so often we find ourselves doing battle over the small issues and alienating our daughters before we can even get to what really matters for their futures—like their self-esteem and their faith. Don't spend time fighting the unimportant battles. If you do, you'll lose the real war.

Instead, be creative, allow uniqueness, and watch your daughter flourish into a delightful young lady.

Great expectations

The second pattern we fall into is one of expectations—those conscious and subconscious ones we've developed long before our daughters entered our lives. Every mother expects her daughter to follow the course she (the mother) knows. But perhaps you are an accountant, and you have an artistic daughter who has never understood coloring within any lines. Or you garden, producing and eating only organic produce, then daily slip into your Birkenstocks, and your daughter wants to become an entertainment lawyer. Imagine a woman who is a politician, always in the limelight, and her daughter wanting to be a stay-at-home mom in the carpool lane.

That's where a mother's counseling in personal creativity must get *really* creative. It must not only ensure that your daughter follows a path of growth in character and principles, but that she also pursues *her own* place in our human race. The one uniquely designed for *her*...not the path *you* choose for her or one of others' expectations.

The girl you are entrusted with is not a clone of you, and she's not her sister or her cousin. She should also not be conformed to the image of what others—your mother, mother-in-law, neighbor, friend—think she should be. This is not to say there might not be invaluable advice from each of those people. But each premise, yours or theirs, must be tempered with the nature of your daughter. Are your expectations based on what's best for your girl—or simply there because it's what you know, what you've been told, and what you're comfortable with?

The girl you are entrusted with is not a clone of you, and she's not her sister, or her cousin.

To do the job of motherhood well, we need to be confident about who we are—even when we don't know how to handle a situation. We need to know what our worth is, what we believe, and how we want to live. If we understand these important issues, it will be easier to guide our daughters to do the same. To perform effectively the duties of a Creative Counselor, we are required to set aside our comfort and do our best to help our daughters follow their own course...all the while maintaining their individuality.

Nellie Cashman is a great example. Though not much has been written about her, I find her series of adventures fascinating. Born in Queenstown, Ireland, she and her older sister, Frances, immigrated to America in 1851, when Nellie was sixteen years of age. Arriving at Boston Harbor, they stayed one year, then boarded a transcontinental train for San Francisco, California.

Nellie signed on as a single woman at the age of twenty-three to a mining troupe as cook and set out for the Cassier Districts in the mountains of Juneau, Alaska. Nellie was a lone, petite, attractive woman, but she held her own. Even in the mining camp the men treated her with dignity and respect. She worked alongside them, cooking and mining, and suffered the same hardship, success, and disappointments they did.

> ## *Nellie was a lone, petite, attractive woman, but she held her own.*
> ## *Even in the mining camp the men treated her with dignity and respect.*

After a year in the mines she left Alaska in the fall to venture into the larger city of Victoria, British Columbia. Upon arrival, she received word that a fierce winter storm had trapped the men she left behind. They had exhausted the major portion of their food and word was they were seriously ill from scurvy and couldn't make their way out.

Nellie purchased potatoes and vegetables, the nutrient-rich foods needed to treat the disease, hired six men to join her expedition, then turned right around and headed back to the mountains. Traversing the ongoing winter storm, Nellie and her hired companions made it back to camp in time to save the lives of her prospecting friends. The mining community's hearts were won, and Nellie became known as "The Angel of Cassair."

Nellie's endeavors included a restaurant in Tombstone, mining in Nevada, and a business in Montana.

In Tombstone, Nellie was well-known for her passion and compassion. Early one morning, she, along with a few men she'd hired, demolished gallows built to hang five murderers. This wasn't done because they were innocent, but because the city was charging admission to the execution. She thought everyone "should die with dignity." After her morning demolition project, she went to the jail and spoke with each man, giving them the opportunity for one last confession. It was their souls that interested her.

Her sister, Frances, was by now widowed and had been left with five children. When Frances was significantly injured from a fall in 1880, Nellie immediately moved to live with her in San Francisco and help take care of the children. Three years later, upon her sister's death, Nellie took it upon herself to become parent and caretaker. Never having married, she moved the children to her home in Tombstone and into her life.

Once back in Tombstone, Nellie again rescued another human. When the price of silver decreased at the Grand Central Mining Company, angry employees were overheard planning the kidnapping and lynching of the mine superintendent. Hearing of their scheme, Nellie paid a visit to the superintendent's home. After a brief stay, she leisurely drove her buggy into town down the main road, then abruptly turned into the railroad station. Jumping out from under a blanket in the back of her buggy was Superintendent Gage. He leaped onto the platform, jumped into the train, and left the city with his life.

After the children were raised, Nellie moved back to Alaska to the territory she loved. This Alaskan legend, known as the first female prospector in this challenging land, lived in a cabin, traveling twelve miles by snowshoes to get her mail. At age seventy she was still mushing (running behind a dog sled) and set a record that year as she mushed her dog sled 750 miles in seventeen days and became champion musher of the world.

I tell you this story because Nellie lived a life I'm pretty sure her mother would never have planned for her. Looking into her sweet daughter's eyes Nellie's mother may have envisioned Nellie playing the piano and raising socialite children while entertaining with her mayor husband.

Like many other little girls of her era, Nellie could have

chosen a domestic life far simpler and much less physically challenging. But that was neither her course nor her character. Hardships and adventures were a mainstay for her as she led the difficult life of a pioneer.

At age seventy she set a record
as she mushed her dog sled 750 miles
in seventeen days and became
champion musher of the world.

And because she did so, lives were changed. Men about to hang were allowed to face their death with dignity. Miners lived to prospect again. Her valiant rescue of the mine superintendent not only saved his life but stopped those who were angry from committing an act they would regret the rest of their lives. Her sisters' children were reared in love and confidence. And Nellie was friend and caretaker to so many more.

Nellie followed a pattern that would have made sense to very few, yet countless lives of those around her were made better by her unexpected choices.

I have absolutely no information on the mother of Nellie Cashman, but I feel fairly confident that she had to have reared her daughters to follow their own course. It is what we must do as well. If we unwittingly force a mold upon our daughter because of what we or culture expects her to be, others will miss being the beneficiaries of things *only your daughter* may be capable to do. But if your daughter is encouraged to fulfill her unique place in this world, she will indeed leave a powerful legacy in the lives around her.

Then you, my friend, will have been a very effective Creative Counselor.

3

WANTED
Time Manager

| Job Description |

Create the principles and systems individuals use to make conscious decisions about the activities that occupy their time. Responsible to develop strategies directing time and motion studies to promote efficient and appropriate utilization of personnel and facilities.

It was Tuesday. My elder daughter sat in the front passenger seat of the car, changing the station on the radio at least once every one minute and thirty-three seconds. You see, she was incapable of listening to any song in its entirety. First verse, chorus, second verse, and she moved on. My younger and her friend were in the back seat talking continuously—about what, I had no idea. I was in the front seat of the car driving, late to their gymnastics class and on my cell phone with calendar in my lap, changing a business meeting I would not make.

I had picked up one child from middle school and the other two from elementary. I was driving back by the middle school because it was the route to the gymnastics class. Logic would have it that I should have gone to the elementary school first, then middle, but of course the school dismissal times would not cooperate with this line of reasoning.

Knowing I was late, yet not paying an enormous amount of attention because I was placing a call, I failed to realize I was back in the school zone. You know—the one where the speed limit drops from 40 mph to 15 mph, when suddenly I heard the abrupt siren. Looking in my rearview mirror, I saw the flashing lights of a police car directly behind me. My heart sunk to the bottom of my stomach; I pulled over and stopped.

The officer walked toward my driver's door, peered in the car, and asked me if I was aware I was driving 40 in a 15. What could I say? I had three children with me and was speeding in a school zone. This zone was designed solely for the protection of children, including those in my car.

Sheepishly I said, "Sorry, I should have known better. I was late for an appointment, and I wasn't paying attention," etc., etc. I had that sick feeling you get when you know you're in the wrong, and you desperately wish for a do-over. My husband would be so frustrated because this is the second ticket I had gotten for speeding in less than one year (and admittedly those were the times I got caught).

I had that sick feeling you get when you know you're in the wrong, and you desperately wish for a do-over.

There go the insurance rates, I thought. I begged, pleaded, and told the officer my entire story, yet I still got the ticket. He felt sorry for me but said there were a lot of speeders in the school zone and the police were on a weeklong crackdown, ticketing everyone they pulled over. He was really nice, doing his job, and absolutely in the right. What else could I have done but meekly take my ticket and say okay?

The police officer did compliment us on all having our seatbelts on. But when I told my husband that to try to soften the blow, it didn't work. He wasn't convinced the seatbelt issue was enough. Perhaps not speeding directly in front of the school would have been a better option. Yet, I was always late.

I was late to pick up my girls, late to dance class, late to business meetings, late to gymnastics, late to dinner. You name it, we were late. We had so much to do. My husband and I were building our businesses, my girls were growing up, and I wanted to be in their lives. I wanted them to have every opportunity, learn all of life's valuable lessons, be brilliant in all endeavors, be involved in everything available to them—and all before they were barely finished with the lemonade stand on the street.

We mothers enroll our daughters in soccer, ballet, modern dance, T-ball, basketball, art, music, and gymnastics. I have always envisioned a cartoon of a child wearing a tutu, with a helmet on their head, number on their shirt, basketball, bat, paint supplies, and musical instrument cradled in their hands while dancing on tiptoe. Who is this child anyway? Are we really expecting any daughter to possess all of those gifts and excel in them by age eight? At the same time they have to attend school…and get straight A's, of course.

Now in hindsight I can emphatically say that we American mothers are officially nuts. The idea that our children should be involved in every activity available is simply wrong. We have created a family circus that exhausts our daughters emotionally, physically, and mentally. And that's not even taking into account *our* state of mind.

The busier we are achieving all of the "programs," the more we miss out on precious time where we could be experiencing life together with our families. Achievement by volume is not achievement—it is distraction. When you involve yourself in every activity, you miss the important ones. Instead of my daughters observing me breaking the law in a constant state of overdoing, I wonder how much better they would have fared if I had taken the time to sit with them and look at the stars? But we were all too weary from our run-around days.

So what's the solution?

Stepping out of the Family Circus Ring

No one wants to be involved in the family circus of exhaustion. But to get out, we have to choose to step out. We must become effective Time Managers. We must slow down, evaluate the schedule objectively, then decide when we want to get into that car and drive. For instance, does that extra trip you're making this afternoon really matter to your daughter's life, success, and well-being in the long run—not to mention your own?

Identify natural talents

The way to manage time well is to first understand your daughter. Every child is talented, but every child does not possess every talent. It's seldom we find the athlete who is also a musician, or the mathematician who is also a painter. It would be unlikely for an engineer to be a politician, or a dancer to be happy sitting in an office. Happiness and fulfillment are found in what we are good at and have a natural inclination toward. Instead of enrolling our children in everything available we serve them better by finding out what their natural talents are before we begin.

To understand the appropriate commitments for your daughter, begin your research by exposing her to as many options as you can. Note that I didn't say *sign her up* for the classes or events. Instead, take her to the soccer games to watch, the concerts and plays to observe, the art museum to look at the paintings. Watch to see when your daughter's eyes light up, listen to her evaluations of the event, and ask if she wants to return to that place. Whether she's excited about the event or not will be obvious. Is she watching raptly, anxious to experience more? Or has she wandered off to find something else to do, wiggled nonstop until intermissions, or drawn on whatever scraps of paper you have in your purse until it's time to go home?

Observation is a key to choosing activities to fill your family time. Does she enjoy tackling her brothers or cousins? When she goes outside to play, is she headed for the basketball goal or the sidewalk with the sidewalk chalk? Maybe she makes art projects out of her food, sees colors at a young age as not merely blue and red but as navy, teal, burgundy, or red-orange. Perhaps she tells wonderful, imaginative stories.

Don't limit your daughter to activities you consider "for her gender." Some girls want a train set or building blocks; if so, perhaps you have a future architect. Some daughters collect bugs, frogs, and pull worms into two halves to see which direction each part slithers. When music plays, does she sing into their hairbrush, hit the pans in the kitchen rhythmically, or dance through the living room? Maybe she acts out scenes from her life—a drama queen before the age of five.

These may not be scientific assessments, but they are Time Manager indicators. A part of your job is to look carefully *before* you sign up. To check out the signs before you cross the metaphorical commitment street—the signs that read WARNING: EXHAUSTION AHEAD, UNDUE PRESSURE FOR ALL, or LEAP ONLY WHEN MASSIVELY PREPARED. If you perform the job of gathering the data on each individual child, you'll choose to sign your daughter up for one class, two classes, or no classes at all.

A part of your job is to look carefully
before *you sign up.*

When mother guilt strikes

I have to warn you, though. There's something unique to *mothers* who are Time Managers. Most people who fulfill these duties of responsible decisions for effective time management sleep well at night. They don't think about what they *didn't* do. We moms, on the other hand, have boatloads of "mother guilt." You know exactly what this is, because there's not a mother on the planet who hasn't experienced it. It's the emotion that hits when your daughter wants to invite a friend over to play on Saturday and her friend's mother informs you there's no opening in her daughter's calendar.

The conversation between mothers goes something like this after school, when you're both in the pickup line at the curb:

You: "Susie would love for Mary to play with her Saturday. They've become such good friends at school."

Other mother: "Oh, sorry she can't play on Saturday. Mary has soccer games. They start so early that Friday night is out as well. What team does Susie play on?"
You (limply): "She doesn't."

Other mother (raising an eyebrow as if reconsidering your motherhood status): "Well, we've been involved with soccer teams since Mary was five. We think she could play pro one day. But she loves basketball as well. Last year her team won state finals, you know. Oh dear, I must get back in my car because I need to be the first in line. Mary has to be at dance in twenty minutes, as well as working on her art project tonight. I can't forget to pack her violin for tomorrow's lesson, either. Is Susie going to take swimming classes, go to the Y camp, or enroll in the community art center this summer? Perhaps the girls could see each other then."

You stutter a reply: "No." Then creatively you add, "Our family will be busy spending our summer helping to design the new space shuttle that will launch from the Kennedy Space Center in the fall. You may know they retired the old one."

As you crawl back to your car, you know you must be a failure as a mom, for running beneath the conversation you hear, "If you were a good mom, Susie would not be available Saturday, either."

Fear hits the middle of your stomach. What if you failed at your motherhood profession because you chose to keep Susie home instead of joining the T-ball team? What if your daughter is a complete failure in life because you have denied her all these activities?

Mother guilt weighs like a brick wall as you sink further into your car seat. You want to be a good mother; you don't want to miss any opportunity for your daughter. What if you alter her success by choosing not to sign up?

Putting Busyness in Perspective

This may come as a surprise to most American mothers, but historically women achieved all kinds of success before we ever invented events for American youth. They became doctors, lawyers, business owners, artists, musicians, and scientists, leading successful, fulfilling lives. Again, one of the most valuable reinforcements of this philosophy is the women of history themselves.

Molly Pitcher

You may have heard of this incredible woman before. She gave water to soldiers on the battlefield during the Revolutionary War for America's independence. She was a tobacco-chewing, hard-talking, tough mama. Yet when the soldiers were losing the battle because of thirst, not only did she bring them pitchers of water, but at one point she took over the loading of the cannon for her husband and shot it herself. He had collapsed from exhaustion; she hadn't.

I doubt that Molly Pitcher had to play T-ball to learn to be a team player.

Betsy Ross

This "flag lady" didn't just sit in her living room, sewing the first United States flag on her lap. She ran her own business, which was hired to make the flag. General Washington met with her, holding a rough, hand-drawn rendition of his concept. Knowing her business like she did, she changed the proportion of the stars, rearranging General Washington's drawing. Then, together, she and the General made a new sketch that was used to tailor the first American flag.

Do you think Betsy Ross's mother signed her up for a year of art lessons in order to accomplish this success? No, the only thing Betsy was probably taught as a little girl was how to sew. The rest came from her creativity, originality, and her business skills.

The price of overachievement

This phenomenon of unrealistic overachievement has been perpetuated in the last fifty years. Sadly, during this same time, the rate of suicide, depression, anorexia, bulimia, and simple exhaustion have climbed astronomically. The win-at-all-costs attitude we've adopted has placed our children on the altar of self-destruction. If the philosophy holds true that busy is better, then our busy children should feel better about themselves...yet they don't. They believe they aren't smart enough, talented enough, pretty enough, or anything enough to feel confident in their self worth.

What's the answer? We need to return to what's simple. To a philosophy that self-esteem is gained by who you are, not what you accomplish. Time management is not merely a time or energy issue; it's an issue of self-esteem and character.

Something so often missed when keeping our daughters so busy is that they don't have time to appreciate the world around them. The beauty is lost when you don't spend the time observing it. The simplicity of a flower's structure and purity of its design can only be seen when you examine it carefully. If your daughter has never studied the night sky and marveled in awe at its wonder, how can she understand the majesty of God and his care for her?

Psalm 8:3-4 says:

When I consider your heavens,
    the work of your fingers,
the moon and the stars,
    which you have set in place,
what is man that you are mindful of him,
    the son of man that you care for him?

In the midst of our constant state of busyness, do we take time to see the stars? Or do we miss out on the wonder?

Time Manager Mothers of today are faced with one final challenge in our technology entrenched society: It's Saturday morning, and you have left your daughter at home playing video games in the family room as you run errands.

Grocery store shopping, dry cleaners, and bank all errands complete, you arrive back at the house...only to realize that your daughter has not moved. She is in the same clothes, in front of the same screen, repeating the movements you observed before you left. Sure, you gave her the list of chores that needed to be accomplished before you returned. But while you were gone, she has been lost in the abyss of gaming for hours, not realizing her morning is gone.

Then there is the Facebook page that daughter of yours is texting her fingers to stubs posting every moment of her existence. Not a good idea on any level. But it is a mainstay in her life nonetheless.

Then, walking toward her room early evening, carrying on a conversation (one-sided), you approach her doorway to find this precious girl staring blindly at a computer screen, grunting responses with no idea that you are in her universe desirous to communicate. It is these moments you realize your daughter has succumbed to a newfound malady: the "I am an electronic zombie losing all track of time or purposeful existence" disease.

In the age of these wonderful new inventions—and they truly are—and the discoveries that inform, entertain, communicate, and enlighten, we have to guard against them taking over. Her cell phone, video game, computer, and any new innovation that enters your home can transform from being a part of your daughter's life to consuming your daughter's life. When technology leaves the realm of a useful tool with a good purpose and becomes the center of her universe, then it's time to set the timer. You may have to limit the smart phone usage, turn off the video game, or take away the computer for a period of time. Just don't be afraid to take whatever steps needed to keep technology in its rightful place.

When technology leaves the realm of a useful tool with a good purpose and becomes the center of her universe, then it's time to set the timer.

So, Time Manager Mom, manage this time consumption as you with every other item your daughter is involved in. You will instruct, monitor, and control. Set the standard, set the limits, and be in charge of the time lost in the world of technology. Do not be afraid to allow her to experience the benefits of these wonderful innovations, just limit their influence. If you succeed at this one, they can glean the meaningful, fun, and educational elements of this great technological age without falling into its consuming and controlling snare.

In our distractions, wherever they come from, we may also miss the people in our lives. There was a time in American history when children were taught relationships and cooperation by being part of a family or community unit, not as part of some other kind of team that changes every few months or every year. And definitely not through social networking. I know many of us don't live in the same town as the rest of our family. But Manager Mom, make time for your children to create relationships in the community you live in with people of other generations. The role once played by grandparents is often lost in our mobile, fragmented society. The wisdom of ages is not shared with our children because the older generation is not included in our daughter's lives. But learning from the previous generation, as well as learning to care for them, wields profound personal results in every next-generation daughter.

My father-in-law stayed with us for five months while recovering from a difficult hip surgery. He couldn't walk without a walker for quite some time and when he did, it was not very far. As a result, he was confined mainly to his room and was very dependent on us while his body healed. Caring for anyone 24/7 is exhausting, no matter how much he or she means to you. There were times my husband and I needed to take a short break.

During one of those instances, we left our daughter Chelsea, seventeen years old at the time, in charge of her grandfather for the evening. When we arrived back home, he was fed (grilled cheese), his medication had been given, his personal needs had been attended to, and even his room was straightened. Chelsea did it all on her own, missing nothing and spending time just talking with him as well!

I couldn't have been more proud. It was one of those "I must be doing okay as a mom" moments, because my daughter had grasped what was important, and she had been responsible and reliable when left in charge. When I told her I was proud of her, she simply shrugged, said, "No big deal," and headed back to her room. A minute later she was on the phone talking with a friend—with music blaring.

Yet somehow in the midst of those teenage, self-absorbed years, my daughter had gained the understanding that time spent caring for someone you love is indeed well spent. My mother side could only sigh and say of my daughter "all is well."

So Mom, become that effective Time Manager. Learn that you manage time; it doesn't manage you. Control the time-consuming distractions in our technological world. Discover who your daughter is, what talents she possesses, and enroll her in *only* the things truly appropriate to her natural gifts and interests. Ignore that mom in the carpool line. She'll soon be hospitalized from exhaustion, and the girls can play together then. Make time with your daughter to experience the beauty of the world around you. Finally, help your daughter know and love the people in her life, those of all generations. This, above all, will show your success as a great Time Manager.

4

WANTED
Media Director

| Job Description |

Oversee the media department with the responsibility of managing the client's media buying and planning needs. Carefully calculate media placement through research and analytical models to determine what is best for the client based on the product/service and the client's goals.

I am sitting in a hotel room in West Hollywood, California. This week I'm here to work as well as visit Loren, my elder daughter, who is pursuing a career in entertainment. That this is her dream didn't come as a surprise to us; she's been on this track since she was in elementary school. Loren is passionate, committed, driven, ambitious, and determined to make her mark in this town.

That in itself is enough to make a mother lose sleep. If you have never visited Los Angeles, California, there is no way to describe what a crazy place this can be. I have traveled throughout the United States of America and visited almost every state in the union as well as an enormous number of cities in all of those states. I've been to Chicago, New York City, Houston, Boston, and Washington, DC, Dallas, Atlanta, as well as every other major metropolitan community we have in this country. Yet there is no place like LA. The capital of film and television sets its own path and its own rules. Some things produced here are great, creative, entertaining, and brilliant. But others? Well, they're not.

As a mother, there are days I find it a challenge to think of my little girl living in this city, knowing the battles in front of her. Those are the days when I have to work hard to keep my fear in check and when I have to let go again—two of a mother's hardest tasks.

When your daughter is young, you tell her happily that there is *nothing* she cannot do. "Follow your dreams, honey!" you say. You know she has been created for a very special place in life and she shouldn't let anything stop her. "The brass ring is yours," you tell her, "so dare to dream!" Those are the days when you use every predictable and trite quote to give her determination.

Then your daughter grows up and has the audacity to take you up on your speech. You find yourself on an airplane with your baby girl, who really is no longer a baby. Flying thousands of miles from home, you deposit her into a place she has chosen to call home. Your task is to help her settle in, give her a huge hug, then load yourself in the rental car and head back to LAX to take the red-eye home. After all you'll be mumbling incoherently to yourself and tears will be streaming the whole eight-hour plane ride, so why not lose sleep too and get a bargain flight?

But the kicker comes when you're sitting in the airplane, surrounded by the snores of other passengers.

"Follow your dreams, honey!" you say.
Then your daughter grows up and has the
audacity to take you up on your speech.

You're thinking, *What was I doing when I said, "Follow your dreams?" Was I completely out of my mind?* Amazing! The one time your daughter listens and trusts what you say brings a result you hadn't thoroughly thought out. I mean, really, thousands of miles from home in this foreign land we call Los Angeles? Couldn't she be just a little closer to home, and in a "safer" location?

But I did mean what I said back then. I wanted her to do exactly that: Follow her dreams.

Now Loren is, and I'm glad. Not glad that she's living in an often angry and sometimes mean world, but that she is willing to take the risk to follow that dream. This city can be tiring—at least to me. So many people, so little grass, and so much concrete.

Not to mention that the interstate highways running through Los Angeles mirror the exact personality of the industry she has chosen—six lanes of bumper-to-bumper traffic heading one direction well exceeding the speed limit until everyone hits their brakes. If they're lucky, the cars come to a simultaneous stop. When they get tied up in traffic, the car owners honk and yell interesting phrases at one another.

In the same way, there's not a lot of grace, mercy, and kindness displayed by the collective front of the entertainment industry. The claim of tolerance is often belied by their reaction when faced with those who don't think like they do. Many are only accepting of those who are completely like-minded and adhere to their standards. They are often creatively and culturally different from the majority of America.

Driving home one night after a difficult day at work, my daughter called me to say, "Mommy, your little girl isn't in Kansas anymore." And we have never even lived in Kansas. Yet her statement was indeed true; this city is not even close to the heartland's values, pace, and philosophies.

An Assembly of Folks

But now that Loren's been in Los Angeles several years, she has met some delightful, loving, and kind people—individuals she cares about very much. Watching her life has reminded me that all we consider a "collective mass" is truly comprised of individuals. No matter what title this group holds, it is not a headless blob but an assembly of folks from every walk of life, from every state in the union.

We parents often spend a lot of time making a ruckus over the entity called *entertainment* and its agenda but forget that the entertainment business is made up of people. Individuals with mothers, fathers, sons, and daughters live in this community and comprise this culture. It is not a collective army of anger. This business is comprised of real people with hopes, dreams, heartaches, births, deaths, with all human needs and wants. Understanding this concept is a key aspect of confidently fulfilling the position of Media Director.

Before we explore these individuals, however, we must recognize that there is not a single stronger source of influence on our daughters than the media. Movies, television, internet, social networking, and music are the most effective and absorbed mediums in our daughters' lives. These engage and change our culture without any notice, creating a gradual and often overlooked effect on the world we live in. Time passes and, if we are not paying attention, we are surprised by the media's content and agenda.

Effecting change

It is our responsibility to neither dismiss nor become afraid of the entertainment world. It only has the power we give it to affect us. It can change and shape us, or we can change and shape it. The choice is ours. What I do know is it must not be ignored.

The interesting part of entertainment is not its effect on us but our effect on it. As I learned through my business life, as well as the life of my daughter, this medium is a collection of humans with a dream to perform, create, and produce. We should not be angry at this group of individuals by what is produced any more than we are at auto-manufacturing workers when our car breaks down or the cell-phone salesman when we can't get a signal. We simply need to address the strengths and weaknesses of this industry to effect change. To do that, a Media Director gathers research and understanding of who comprises the industry prior to making "buys" for our client—in this case, our daughters.

So step back and take a different view. Instead of looking at the world of entertainment as if it is the threatening "blob" from the 1958 horror and sci-fi film, understand that you are in control. In fact, each of us has all of the control we choose to accept. But to make this task manageable, you must first understand the people involved in media and how we affect them. To begin, they come in two pretty simple forms, the performers and the behind-the-scenes folk.

> ## *Each of us has all of the control*
> ## *we choose to accept.*

Performers

Performers are drawn to their profession out of need—to deliver art and to be liked and accepted. The talents that make them want to be on the performance platform are couched and driven by that need. They want to please, delight, entertain, and gain the attention of an audience. And they need to accomplish this for their personal satisfaction as well as insuring that they remain a viable part of an industry that brings the world the arts (not to mention bringing home a paycheck). When an audience doesn't embrace a work, a performer is extremely unfulfilled. A theater without an audience or a song without a listener is a sad creation.

The success of performers can be defined in several ways.

There is the immediate success of a job appreciated by an

audience, reviewers speaking accolades in print or on television about an artist's performance.

There are the awards presented by peers.

Yet the single most visible determinant of success is sale of records or music downloads, concert tickets, television ratings, or box office revenue. By this barometer the companies that fund the projects will determine their continued involvement with the artist. If a performer doesn't make money for a company, they find themselves no longer with a job. Their passion is not fulfilled, nor is their opportunity still available.

Behind the scenes

As an observer of the entertainment world, I've seen that the people behind the scenes drive a lot of the content. They often have an agenda and purpose in what they produce. But the fact remains that if they want to continue working, they have to succeed financially. No matter what the agenda is, without financial success they cannot—and I repeat cannot—continue in their business.

Who creates the media's financial success? We do. It's pretty simple. It may take a couple of bad movies, low music sales or TV ratings, but the outcome is inevitable. If their projects don't make money, they are out of work.

> *Who creates*
> *the media's financial success?*
> *We do.*

That means we, the consumers, are the biggest influencers of entertainment. It is up to you to determine who will win the audience and what kind of productions you will support. You can choose for them not to influence you and your daughter. I'm not saying boycott, just *choose*. Be the one who directs what your daughter hears and sees, and when she sees it. Be informed and aware of the content of movies, for example, before you allow your daughter to see the movie with a friend.

This job of Media Director is one of the most demanding. A large amount of time is required to succeed at this position. You must spend the energy and time to research what entertainment is offering your family. When was the last time you watched MTV, researched movie titles or television shows, or listened to music targeted to your daughter? Do you know the iTunes list of Top Songs and Top Albums being downloaded, the current Billboard Top 100, or the Top Ten Box Office Movies? Which YouTube videos are being viewed the most? Are you aware of what determines the definition of G, PG, PG13, and R-rated movies? What language is allowed, what sexual content is included in these productions?

It's so easy for time to fly by…and suddenly you find yourself in a world that is your daughter's but one you seemed to completely miss.

It's All About Oversight

It wasn't that long ago when you and your daughter began your life together. Looking back, the memories are sweet, aren't they? It was a special day, the day that you and your sweet daughter met for the first time.

Whether you birthed your daughter or adopted her, the day you brought your child home was the one you'd dreamed about, pondered, feared, and anxiously looked forward to. It was merely a few short days before this, most likely, that you saw her beautiful face, held her hand, and changed a diaper for the first time. This precious bundle was your girl—she was real! Yet, before she was born, she seemed like a dream, a kick, indigestion, discomfort, a foot in your ribcage, or a concept and a hope in the midst of a stream of adoption paperwork.

Perhaps a few months into the pregnancy you went to the doctor with expectations, then saw her on the ultrasound. Well, what you saw was a blur—a foot, a head, or some other body part. But as the technician explained what you were looking at, your eyes marveled at seeing your wonderful daughter on film for the very first time. You knew then she was *your baby,* even if, to others, she looked like just a fuzzy blob!

For those of you who adopted, you saw a photo of a child...and fell in love. The reams of paperwork and months of preparation fell away as you stared transfixed at the tiny photo from another state or from overseas. Or perhaps you were allowed to see the child right after birth.

You couldn't wait to welcome that child into your arms.

Those first days home

Finally the day arrived—no fanfare, no parades, only tears and agony until you first saw her treasured face. Then one look at that sweet and precious baby and you knew: you would do *anything* to care for this little one.

You couldn't wait to welcome that child into your arms.

You learned her cry, her yawn, her squiggly face that you swore was a smile but was probably indigestion. You fed her, changed her diaper, and had the gracious help of the hospital or adoption staff to make sure you weren't messing up too badly. They were there to help you do most things right. So being a mom didn't seem that difficult—at least not in that environment.

But then came the time to take her home. This was the day to begin your life together—your real life. You dressed her carefully in the special clothes picked out for her trip home. The car seat was already in the car waiting to be filled—after all, you set it up a month ago in anticipation of the happy event. You bundled her for cold even though it was 80 degrees outside, fearing some germ would touch her new life. With daughter in your arms, suitcase already delivered to the car, you are wheeled out of the hospital through the automatic door by some precious volunteer who tells you what a beautiful girl yours is. Although you realize that volunteer has seen a million babies, ugly ones at that, you know they are right this time. Your daughter *is* beautiful.

The car seat is triple checked to make sure the belt is sufficiently tight. You strap your treasure in for the first time and check all of the buckles over thoroughly before you get into the car for the drive home. Opening the front door, you climb into the passenger's seat to turn around and look at your daughter, making sure she is ready for the journey. In panic, you realize she is facing the back of the car, can't see you, may be frightened, and you just need to get back there with her. So you roll out of the front passenger door and make your first mother move by sitting in the back by the car seat so she won't be scared. You don't even notice that she sleeps the whole way and would have been fine.

The drive home is uneventful, her first car ride safe and secure. She has arrived home healthy, with no accident or disaster on the way, and is only whimpering a little. The motion of the car seems to fascinate her, then lull her to sleep. Pulling in your driveway, you wait until the car comes to a complete stop, turns off, and then you begin unbuckling her from her car seat.

What a wonderful moment when you enter your home with her for the first time. She is your baby girl, and she is home!

Now the work begins. You change her diapers, rock her to sleep, and feed her every few hours' day or night. To say you are tired is a vast understatement. Pondering when you had your last night of real sleep, you stare straight ahead. *Months,* you decide. It was months before she was born when you slept a whole night; now it looks as if you may never sleep again. You begin to panic.

And that precious little girl of yours can certainly cry. We're not talking delicate whimpers; these are earth-shattering wails, and they don't end. Even the neighbors are covering their ears.

It looks as if you may never sleep again.
You begin to panic.

It's midnight. She's screaming again, and it seems nothing will make her stop and go to sleep. So here you are one more night, buckling your sweet child in the car seat, counting on the fact that car motion still lulls her to sleep. This time you quadruple check the restraints, because you're so tired you aren't sure you did it right. At 1:00 a.m. you find yourself driving around the block to get some peace. At 1:15 you have pulled back into the garage and are snoring in the front seat of the car, treasuring whatever rest you can get, while your daughter is sleeping in the car seat. You dare not move, or those precious sleeping minutes may be interrupted. That car is the best bed you've slept in for what seems like an eternity.

But it's not only the lack of sleep. It's also the feeding.

How many times can a baby be hungry? Heavens, it seems you are constantly preparing formula or nursing; the process is never-ending. No breaks for you to eat a nice dinner yourself. You dream of the day your daughter can sit up in her high chair, put the food into her own mouth, and chew. Just the simple stuff—macaroni and cheese, spaghetti, chicken pieces, vegetables...anything that would be served at the family table.

When will she be ready? you wonder. First it's the mushy cereal, then the mushy fruits, then the mushy meats. I think whoever invented mushy meat must have been having a majorly "off" day—such disgusting stuff. But real food—the bits of fruit, vegetable, and breads that can come from meals prepared for the rest of the family—doesn't come for months. You're exhausted by the process of trying to get the little bits into your baby.

Mmm...maybe she can handle table food sooner than other babies, you think. *She seems pretty smart. She might be quicker at everything. Let's give table food a try.*

It seems like it would be a great relief to fast-forward through some of those first steps, doesn't it? After all, if you start her earlier on table food, you can rest a bit more. So really, why not?

Fast-forwarded kids in a media-heavy world

Wrong! Nothing your child grows into being able to handle can or should be fast-forwarded. That includes food, crossing the street, tying her own shoes, brushing her own teeth, or learning algebra. Life is to be experienced by your daughter when she is ready and has been taught and is prepared to handle it. Even if you're tired and it looks like so much work to make sure she isn't exposed to something before she is ready, you have to protect her. Even when you are weary, you must remember that other people have an agenda contrary to yours. If you are tired and don't want the battle, you still cannot give in.

There is no place truer of this concept than the world of entertainment. There is some fare in the entertainment world that no one is old enough to consume and simply shouldn't be experienced. But there is a lot of the entertainment world that has merit, value, and even pure distraction from the mundane side of life. Yet music, movies, the internet, and television has a time and a place in your daughter's life. Knowing what and when that is becomes crucial for a mother rearing girls in our media-heavy world.

I'm not sure where we got the idea that it's okay to let our children be exposed to the world of entertainment without guidance and instruction. They need our oversight. As in all things, this requires balance. We must protect but not overprotect. We cannot shelter them from everything entertainment offers. If we attempt to shield all exposures, they will be sent off to college ill-prepared to handle what is thrust upon them from this medium, because media is at its height of influence in these years. Yet as our daughters grow, we allow the world of entertainment into their lives well before they are ready to handle it.

My father was a wonderful teacher. He wasn't an educator by profession, but an effective instructor to his impetuous daughter, me. I know I drove my daddy crazy because I was always following roads that made no sense. But while I was paving my own path, my father was determined to teach me his values.

We were not allowed to use any profanity in our home. I don't believe I ever heard my father say one single off-color word or joke. He loved language and words of all types but not those. In fact, he would make us learn words on a regular basis; we would pronounce new words for him, spell them, define them, and pronounce them again for him. We did this repeatedly until he seemed satisfied that we had gained one more vocabulary word in our repertoire. But I digress. The point is that the words he would not allow us to say we were entirely aware of.

> ## *While I was paving my own path,*
> ## *my father was determined*
> ## *to teach me his values.*

When I was fourteen, traveling in our family car, I convinced my daddy to turn on the radio station I wanted to listen to. On came the song "Sunshine," by Jonathan Edwards. It was a fun little ditty I loved to sing along with. While I was happily singing the lyrics in the back seat, my father, sitting up front, was actually listening. Most of the time a girl would be delighted that her father was listening to her musical ability. But this time he was listening not only to me but to the *lyrics.*

Suddenly the volume knob was turned completely down.

Startled, I looked up, quit singing, and realized that Daddy was in control. He simply said, "Sweetie, keep singing." Oh brother, I was in trouble. I wanted to do anything but continue the next line. But my father wasn't a man to give up when he was making a point. He said again, "Keep singing." So I had to complete the next line in the chorus, "But he can't even run his own life, I'll be damned if he'll runs mine."

No one had to say another word. I was nailed! I had been caught using a word unacceptable to my father, and even if it was just a song lyric, that wasn't allowed. It may seem like a minor offense to you, but I'll never forget that moment. Heart racing, palms sweating, I knew the music I was listening to was not okay with my daddy.

Why did my dad do that? you ask. He wanted to make sure I didn't accept something he didn't approve of just because my culture did. He wanted me to think through my choices and actions to make sure they aligned with the values he was teaching me. Now that's a smart parent. For me, it was a lesson well learned.

While your daughter is gaining knowledge of the medium, it is your job, as Media Director, to guide her. If you know your rules, understand completely the world of entertainment and the culture it is creating for your daughter's consumption, you will be able to do so wisely, like my dad did. You should *never* accept from entertainment a lifestyle diametrically opposed to the one you are creating for your daughter.

Are film ratings enough?

We gain much of our information on films from the rating systems. They are designed to tell us what age is appropriate for our children to see various movies. But the irony is that no one knows who determines the standards for these ratings. The members of this board are anonymous. Never having met a single one of those people, why should you use their standards as your standards?

Have you ever once in your life made a decision suggested to you by a group of people you didn't know? If you didn't know who they are, where they live, or what their life criteria is, would you really trust them with a key decision in your life?

The rating system is no different. It may indeed be correct, but the only way to know is to investigate the content yourself and make your own determination of the age-appropriate material that would be delivered to your daughter.

Never accept from entertainment
a lifestyle diametrically opposed to the one
you are creating for your daughter.

Also, *you* are the only one who truly knows your particular daughter. Each child is influenced differently in life. Sensitivities in your first child will not be the same in any other children you may have down the road. All children are individually responsive to input and should be treated that way when determining what appropriate fare is.

But let me be quick to say that it would be equally wrong to completely shelter your daughter from the world around her. Just as you fed her the appropriate food at the appropriate time, there is an exposure to information that is vitally important under your instruction.

If you completely protect your daughters from anything in the world outside your home, they will be unprepared to handle it when they go it alone. And they *will* go it alone. So they must be allowed to experience entertainment through your eyes.

You may say they should never see an R-rated movie, and at a young age this is infinitely true. But teens can be impacted positively by films such as *Schindler's List, Saving Private Ryan,* and *The Passion of Christ.* Is it appropriate for them to view the harshness of reality in film form? This is something you, as the parent, have to decide. If it is appropriate for your daughter, and the content important and beneficial to educating her, then the media should be considered. But it must also be an educated, well-thought-out decision.

Knowledge and understanding of entertainment content is always the goal of a Media Director. If we moms allow all influences into our daughters' lives, they will accept lifestyles and situational ethics that are contrary to what we want them to learn. But if we insulate them from all influence, they will be ill prepared to make decisions independent from the insulation of their family instruction. The key is to stay involved, knowledgeable, and balanced in their consumption of the arts.

Influences from the inside

The fact that the world of entertainment terrifies so many in Middle America stunts the opportunity for change. This fear is simply out of step with the need that exists. We must be willing to influence media from the inside by encouraging participation in entertainment and the arts by our daughters and like-minded individuals who are passionate to be part of this community. When we disagree with the entertainment we are given, why not act to change it—instead of running from it in fear?

The key is to stay involved, knowledgeable, and balanced.

What if your daughter is one of those people destined to be a part of that change in media? Then let her go do it! Her talents and gifts may cry out in that direction, as our daughter Loren's did. Never let your fear deter your daughter from her destined path. If you have worked extremely hard the first eighteen years of her life to help her be the solid young woman she is capable of being, you have given her the tools she needs to change the media industry—

for the good. Why not make it better for her children, and her children's children?

Opening Minds to Possibilities

Television and film has also positively influenced young women, opening minds to possibilities not found in the small towns they grow up in.

When I was young, I wanted to be Emma Peale—a British spy on the late 1960s television program *The Avengers*. Emma was beautiful, sophisticated, and hip. She had a great accent and could beat up any bad guy or girl who came along. She saved countries, friends, and foiled evil, with never a hair out of place. I really wanted to be a spy: travel the world, defeat evil, and wear great clothes. Not a thing wrong with those dreams. Though I didn't do what Emma did, just watching her made me believe anything was possible. That can't be all bad for a young girl in America.

When I was young,
I wanted to be Emma Peale.
Travel the world, defeat evil,
and wear great clothes.

My mother's culture began wearing their hair partially covering their eyes because an actress named Veronica Lake looked good that way. Then, in the 1950s, young girls went bleach-blonde because of Marilyn Monroe. Many boys wanted to wear leather jackets to be like James Dean. In the 1960s we surfed and wore bikinis because of Frankie Avalon and Annette Funicello, then became flower children by the 70s. Girls would be seen in knit caps like Ali McGraw in *Love Story*, then Annie Hall style with hats and suspenders. The 80s found us *Saturday Night Fever* dancing through the era with John Travolta and flashdancing with

Jennifer Beals. The 90s reminded us of historical moments of valor through *Saving Private Ryan* and *Braveheart*. After the turn of the century, movie entertainment grew exponentially as viewers were reintroduced to classic books like *Lord of the Rings*, and *Chronicles of Narnia* in film form. Movie-watching became the mainstay for Friday and Saturday night entertainment. That's what you did with your friends, with your date, or in your own family room.

Music is no different. The war songs from our parents' generation gave them courage and respite from difficult times. "Praise The Lord and Pass the Ammunition" was sung to me by my mother, but I never did get it. Praise the Lord and bullets— all in the same song? But for her generation I believe it brought resolve and resilience in an extremely hard time. Music has brought racial and political change as well as portraying love, loss, and celebration. It both commiserates on our sadness and marks occasions in which we delight.

I am a huge believer in the arts. Creative endeavors are magnificent! They provide color in a black-and-white world, and we should adamantly support them. Entertainment is a medium originally created to inspire and uplift. Let's do our best to make it become that again. We can succeed in pursuing that path by determining what is best for our daughters to partake in and purposefully avoiding what is not.

We must encourage our creative daughters to forge their roads within these industries. By their participation, they can change the culture in which we live.

If you take this job to successfully review and manage media, becoming a killer Media Director, your daughter will be effectively guided, your daughter's friends will be amazed at what you know, and future generations will be changed.

5

WANTED
Academic Advocate

| **Job Description** |

Advocate on behalf of students in education programs and services. Responsible to work with student and the academic system to help individuals select, outline, and achieve educational and developmental goals.

Pick up a newspaper or turn on the television and you'll be confronted with a story on our failure in education. Students who can't read, low test scores, classes that are too large, subjects that are unlearned all seem to be evidence of a fruitless system. The perceived need for money or more teachers, opening new schools and closing old ones, standardized testing for students and testing of teachers echo through the ongoing debate. We argue, set goals, make plans, spend more money; then argue, set goals, make plans, and spend more money again. Yet the stories appear, and the goals remain unmet.

There has to be an answer; we can't surrender our daughters to a failed system. We can't surrender any children to a failed system that is tasked to provide the education for future success. By allowing our children to remain in a quagmire that does not educate, we defeat the purpose of schools altogether.

Such failure of education cannot be allowed to continue.

Let me suggest a mothering job that would *ensure* our students get educated. And the effects of this job will be best accomplished when compounded with other mothers committed to the same position. Envision with me what would terrify any school board in any county in America: a group of mothers—relentlessly determined to improve the school system their children attend—enter the chambers for the scheduled meetings. They listen, respond, and demand what is in the best interest of the *student,* not being concerned with the interest of the boards, nor the administration, nor even the teachers.

No other human is more motivated than we moms when it comes to educating our children. We are a powerful group with enormous ability and influence that enables us to do this job well, so we should use it. To make sure students are being taught, we mothers must be their Academic Advocate.

No other human is more motivated
than we moms when it comes
to educating our children.

Some years ago I watched a television interview with Phylicia Rashad, the actress who so brilliantly played the role of the mother, Clair Huxtable, on the classic television program *The Cosby Show.* This program aired in the early years of the daytime talk show *The View* and centered around a discussion regarding the plight of children in American education. The lack of learning, hope, and direction seemed rampant to the interviewer, Barbara Walters, and she was seeking a perspective from an actress she obviously admired. Anticipating the normal response of government intervention, new programs, and money undergirding the system, I was surprised at what I heard from Ms. Rashad.

She stated that no one is as effective in a child's life as their parents. Not educators, politicians, no one. Interestingly, she didn't

71

differentiate between the needs of children born into wealth or poverty. In fact, when asked, she stated that both the wealthy parent and the impoverished parent are capable of great good or great harm. I wholeheartedly concur. Her focus was far from the normal platitudes that give responsibility to others, but she placed that burden directly upon the parents, stating that we should be "our children's advocate."

We are to be the one who represents and stands for our child's welfare. We are not to await help from anyone else; it is *our* duty to change for our children what needs to be changed.

To truly do this well, we have to understand the specifics of this job. I love the synonyms of the word *advocate.* An advocate is a supporter, backer, promoter, believer, activist, campaigner, and sponsor. The platform of education is the right one for us to be that person in our daughter's life.

It is our duty to change for our children what needs to be changed.

We can address and debate all kinds of issues about education, but when we put our daughter on that school bus for the first time, we don't want to waste our time or hers. Our girls are boarding that bus to receive an education, nothing less. The goal must be to acquire tools to be a productive member of our society...simply to learn for life.

There is a system in place for that purpose—the American Education system—but it is far from perfect, and each school is an individual challenge. Knowing what you want for your daughter is one thing. But evaluating your school, then supporting and changing it where needed requires the activist in each of us.

As mothers we fear the influences in our girls' lives—sexual pressure, driving a car, alcohol, and drugs, to name a few. We would never allow our daughters away from us seven hours a day with no real understanding of what they are doing, who is caring for them, how they are being affected, and what good is coming from those hours. But we often do this with their education.

Is your daughter being taught what she needs to learn to become a woman of purpose? Do you know the teachers who are educating her? Are these educators instilling merely academics, or also theories and philosophies in their curriculum that might go against your values? Do the academics required of your daughter fit the needs and talents she possesses?

Building Your Knowledge Base

My husband and I have built two homes, one office building, and remodeled a third home. The tasks each time were daunting. From beginning to end they required a lot of effort on our part. Imagine when building a home that you meet a person someone else sent into your life to take care of this task for you. You spend forty-five minutes in a room with that person along with twenty-five other couples he is building for as well, and he tells the whole group how the year is going to go. After that brief meeting, you give him your cash, then drive away, never seeing the builder again until you return to your site and the house is completed.

It's preposterous to think you'd leave a project like that with just anyone who pulled up in a pickup truck removing their tool belts from their vehicles to begin labor on your home. You haven't seen the detailed plans. You don't know where the windows are located, let alone the room sizes, plumbing fixtures, and electrical outlets. If you wanted to make sure your home was being built well, you'd meet and interview the workman, define the role they would play, and sign a contract way before the first piece of dirt was moved to lay the foundation.

You'd also need to be confident that these people knew their trade—that they were prepared to build the home you wanted with the materials and craftsmanship you expected. You would never want to drive up to your completed home, crafted by people you know nothing about, and find the surprises: the leaking roof, the clogged sinks, and the cracked flooring.

But in the building of the knowledge base of our daughters, we do exactly that. We don't know the teachers, the classes, or the education they are receiving. We have a forty-five-minute meeting at the beginning of the year and return at the end of the school year to pick up our children for summer vacation.

Okay, so there are parent-teacher conferences if needed. But if your child is not making waves, you may not get called in. Perhaps you attend a play, sporting event, or a concert. But as a parent, that is not enough. You must be involved in the substance of education, supporting and defining it along the way.

Three Fault Lines in Education

To do this well, you must understand the three fault lines in education:

- The academic focus lacks understanding of the diversity of human talent.
- The culturally relevant education has an emphasis on feeling and philosophy, not fact.
- The system doesn't offer a practical education—one that meets the needs of day-to-day life.

Every student should be given the opportunity and be expected to read, write, and master math problems. Every student should be given the opportunity and expected to learn discipline in study, achievement and mastery of skills, knowledge of factual history to understand their world, and a view of their country's inception, purpose and privilege. We should also understand when reviewing our school teachers and school administrators that not all are incompetent, agenda-ized, or uncompassionate.

My daughters have had the privilege of being taught by many teachers who are both compassionate and valiantly committed to their craft. The instruction Loren and Chelsea received from these teachers was magnificent and will forever enrich their lives. I will stand and defend these warriors in education as ardently as I will work to change a flawed system. Recognizing and supporting the successes in education are as important as addressing the faults. As we examine the changes we can make, let's do it with reason.

Fault line #1: The inability to educate the diverse.

Diversity is a word bandied about in contemporary conversations, but that's not the general definition of diversity I'm talking about. Diversity is not about race, gender, height, weight, or even nose size. It's about humans who have many and differing talents, gifts, and abilities—all wonderfully complementary! Math, English, and science aren't the only talents we find in girls. Humans possess all kinds of delightful, creative, and unique abilities—talents that need attention to be developed.

I was a mere fourteen years of age when I made my own education disclaimer. Not understanding at the time why I did it, I found myself actively making my own path.

"No, Bob Hinkle isn't my brother."

You see, my name was Darlene Hinkle, so logic would have it that somehow we came from the same gene pool. Yet this is the sentence that began my freshman year of high school. I said it to every educator at my high school. These were the teachers who had made a commitment to educating students, opening their eyes to possibilities and infusing them with knowledge. I'm sure they thought I was truly crazy when the first thing out of my mouth after raising my hand for attendance was: "In case you're curious, I don't know Bob Hinkle."

In every class I attended I made this proclamation. On my first visit to the school office I told the secretaries at their desks, "Bob Hinkle, you know him? Well, I don't." I'm quite sure I even sang it down the halls just to make sure it was understood. You see, these people frightened me. They had expectations I had absolutely no intention of meeting.

I have this older brother, four years my senior. I love him very much, but he was, and is, really smart. Bob was the kind of guy who of course took Calculus and Trigonometry because he could; perhaps he actually enjoyed them. When he went to college, he majored in engineering, experimenting in which kind he would like to pursue—electrical, architectural, aeronautical, civil, and whatever other engineering they offered that I hadn't a clue about.

Bob can read almost anything and retain the most profound information. He is one of the most well-read, well-studied, and able to approach every subject from a basis of knowledge humans I know. He is also gracious, kind, and a great guy.

But in high school I saw all of this intelligence as a stumbling block in the path I wanted to take. I didn't want the pressure of having to be smart too, so I chose the easy road. I lied. Bob had already graduated, so it was a simple statement. I told myself I could easily pull this off and make my own path to the land of higher education. It was also the path of least resistance.

I didn't want the pressure of having to be smart too, so I chose the easy road. I lied.

I'm a person who is focused (my husband calls it stubborn), yet I say I'm merely tenacious. I don't give up on commitments. While in high school I made commitments. They included insuring that there were enough study halls in my school day to never bring work home. I graduated actually having achieved this goal. I decided to, at all costs, avoid the intense math and sciences, choosing instead to take music, art, psychology, composition, and any class known as a "fluff course." Such courses were my education mainstay. I only took what I had to in order to get my degree and college admittance because my parents wanted to make sure I didn't forsake all life options by my "tenacious" commitments.

My senior year was the greatest. My school had a work study program that was actually a very practical form of education. But for me, it was prison furlough. I could get out of school before noon and go to a job where I was paid real money at the same time I was getting high school credit.

What a plan! Leave school early, eat lunch wherever you want, and go to a job that isn't that hard because the people are kind and don't expect much from a high school senior. And while working, I was completing my high school education. Then, as an added bonus, I got to take a midday break from my work when my boyfriend could meet me and take a thirty-minute ride on his motorcycle. Life was good.

All of this information was kept secret from my daughters for a very long time. Did I want them to follow in their mother's footsteps? I think not.

Was it the best plan for a high school education? Not even.

Did my deceit lead to my betterment? What do you think?

Yet traditional education isn't right for everyone. I'm not excusing my own choices in high school, but I realize now that they weren't all wrong on my part. I was not Bob Hinkle. I was Darlene Hinkle. Math was not my major talent; I was creative. While some students were intrigued by the possibilities of math formulas, I was visualizing an entire play. I was creating and sewing extremely unique items of clothing and then daring to wear them in public. Music played in my mind constantly.

While I'm not recommending we allow our daughters to take the path of least resistance, I am recommending that as Academic Advocates it is our job to make sure they receive the education appropriate to their talents. When they have to take a predetermined number of math, science, and English classes for college entrance, what time do we allow for the arts? And time isn't the only issue. The lack of variety of programs in our schools is a disservice as well. When looking for jobs that require creativity, you may be surprised at how numerous they are.

Traditional education isn't right for everyone.

In the world of television and film there are hundreds of jobs for the individuals possessing specific talents. Screen-writing, acting, directing, producing, editing, and operating cameras are all careers to fulfill that part of the entertainment world. There are talent agents, television network employees, film company personnel, animators, costumers, musicians, set designers, and special effects creators that all take part in the finished product we see on the small and large screen.

Then you take the world of music. Songwriters, publishers, musicians, studio engineers, managers, performers, singers, record company employees, publicists, studio owners, album cover designers, video producers, directors, and scores of others are essential to the creation and distribution of the music we listen to.

We can't forget about art, photography, theater, clothing design, books, and the lists go on. Our world would be sterile without creativity. How boring buildings would look if they were left only to minds filled with actualities, not possibilities. Design or art is such a vital part of our world. We have to ask ourselves if we are nurturing the creative talents as much as we are nurturing the scientific and mathematic talents. We spend so much time working on the brain we lose the heart and soul.

My niece, Shanna, is smart, really smart. She took her first ACT test when she was thirteen and tested better than most high school seniors. She has gone on to score in high school the perfect 5 on advanced placement tests in mathematics. She is the academically off the chart member of our family.

Through the years we took a lot of trips together. Spring breaks were some of our favorites. Our family owned this big red conversion van. It was great for traveling, because it was full size, with room for up to seven people. All back and middle seats had headphone jacks that would attach to the television, CD player, or car radio. That meant each kid traveling with us could choose her own entertainment. Life was wonderful during those trips because the front seats, where we adults sat, were quiet. Not the normal "when are we getting there?", "how much longer?", or other questions when you still have miles to go until you reach your destination. We adults could relax, talk to each other, or nap (if we weren't the driver), and just focus on the road ahead.

My girls would be busy with their music or movies. But Shanna? She'd often be found working in a book—and not just any book, but a math brain-teaser book, designed to make math more challenging, complex, and difficult. Shanna loved them. To me, these books represented work—a painful exercise not ever undertaken by choice, something to avoid at all costs. But to Shanna, it was fun.

God wired Shanna's brain to love math, and I'm so glad he did. Without brains like hers, the creative people would not have the cameras, computers, studios, electronics, and all the other types of technology that are necessary in today's world to create and distribute their art. And if it were not for the creative people, the mathematicians and engineers would be limited in the need for their innovations. Their world would lack color. To build a computer only for math or science and not for graphic art, image generation, animation, editing, or music recording would be developing a sterile technology.

Difficult math and science subjects are good for those, like Shanna, who are destined for those careers. But never should they be the only life route, nor should they be the only praise-worthy endeavor in education. If your creative daughter makes Cs or Ds in math and is working her very best, then her best should be good enough. If her talents are creative, they should be applauded, as well as nurtured and developed. As in every part of life you must identify your daughter's talents, understand them, and support her. Never let traditional education defeat your daughter.

If your creative daughter makes Cs or Ds in math and is working her very best, then her best should be good enough.

Recognizing there are students like Shanna and students like I was and providing for varied talents is crucial to a well-rounded education system. It's also imperative knowledge for advocating effectively for your daughter. Redirecting some academic emphasis and requirements from the core subjects to the creative subjects is one necessary step toward a diverse education. It's also one area that the effective Academic Advocate relentlessly pursues with the school board.

Fault line #2: The emphasis on feeling, philosophy, and cultural relevance instead of instruction of facts.

I love the statement of Sherwood Anderson, renowned author of American literature in the early 1900s, regarding education. "The whole object of education is…to develop the mind. The mind should be a thing that works." That's certainly simple enough, isn't it? Yet we are led to believe the education system is lofty and above common man…when it is not. If the brain works, the information provided in teaching form should be enough. It should be not be interpreted, diffused, or in any way construed as anything other than simple fact. The mind doesn't need development; it only needs fact-based instruction.

I recently noticed a change in education when it comes to

80

history. It has evolved into a non-messy and content-selective subject in our school system. When history is cleaned up and sanitized, it is no longer history. The study of our human past is filled with faults, mistakes, and complicated humans—those who did great wrong and those who did inordinately right. History is filled with the evil acts and the valiant acts of humankind. Putting history under a foggy lens, trying to make it politically correct or slanted toward cultural justice, is a disservice to our children. To learn life lessons, you have to know and understand past mistakes and the consequences of those actions.

The educators that have chosen to provide a culturally relative education are missing the reality of what education is. Learning all information just as it is and gaining insight from that knowledge enables the student to determine how she wants to live.

Culturally relevant education is based upon the thinking that the education system would provide a relevant education, an education society deems to be useful and needful.

Following World War II American education strayed from pure education (the simple facts) to the functions of solving society's problems—poverty, pollution, urban unrest, crime, and any other malady the institution felt needed addressing. This began mainly in the universities of the time because government grants were being given out to professors who taught classes on how to remedy the cultural ills of society. Each time a social ill was addressed by the professor, the possibility of an infusion of government dollars came into that department. This climate created a diversion from the teaching of factual information to the *interpretation* of that information. No longer were the instructors in place for, or even paid for, the teaching of only fact. Instead, they became entitled and even obligated to dispense opinion to the students.

Therefore, amidst education fact, one will find information spun to support a professor's theory, correct a perceived wrong, and change the views of the listeners. What's wrong with that? It's opinion, an individual's thought. The conclusions can be based on false assumptions, from a background that is culturally different from your own; yet, coming from an instructor, they are dispensed with authority. A student relies upon a teacher for correct, unbiased information—not theory. Theory should only be presented as a line of reasoning that is in no way provable or is potentially inerrant, not as conclusive.

The issue with culturally relative education is that it is backwards. Conclusions are taught prior to instilling the information that led to development of the conclusion. The *students* are the ones who should form the conclusions, not their instructors.

If taught in science about the world of botany, without the teacher editorials that usually go along with it, the student who loved the beauty of plants and the scientific interrelation of the vegetative life would naturally follow the path of maintaining and protecting plant life. Now that's ecology in motion!

The students are the ones who should form the conclusions, not their instructors.

If taught the messiness of history with slavery, genocide, battle, and taught about the defenders of freedom, the liberator students who are activists by nature would find their cause and purpose. Equality would be advanced, injustice would be addressed, and the defenseless defended. Prior to the culturally relative period of education many wrongs were righted, many downtrodden lifted up, and human compassion advances made because a need was seen and a purposed heart was ignited.

The education system then found itself advancing forward from trying to answer corporate problems to addressing the therapeutic needs of the students. Many educators felt the need to cope with the students' "identity crisis" and resolve emotional conflict. This led to an aggressive thrust toward a student's self-awareness—feeling good about who you are and achieving for yourself in this culturally relevant education system.

At first glance, it sounds good, doesn't it? You don't want your daughter to feel badly about herself, do you?

Well, yes, you do. Feeling badly about yourself—knowing you can achieve more, be kinder, and work harder—is part of improving as a human. Self-disappointment is an important emotion. Your daughter will be better if she thinks she needs to. While teaching the feel-good philosophy, schools don't promote kindness, humility, compassion, personal ethics, and integrity. They instead create a selfish atmosphere where the mind and self is valued over all other achievements.

You may think it's not the schools' purpose to teach humility, but why not? They are teaching pride. And what about ethics? Shouldn't the concept of ethics be interwoven in achievement? There is a right and wrong. There are truth and lies. These principles must be understood as the core of human achievement, or all other instruction taught will fail miserably.

If your daughter doesn't do her homework it's not okay. If she doesn't study for the test, she should receive a failing grade, even if doesn't make her "feel good." After all, she earned it. Personal responsibility in education teaches humility. Consequences for actions are necessary for real-life advances.

Fault line #3: The lack of instruction to prepare the student for life in the real world.

This is why it's so vital to you, Mom, to be your daughter's Academic Advocate. Historically, education has been the only means to a life that would otherwise be unlikely. It's the tunnel from poverty to position, from lack of accomplishment and failure to success. For many, it's the only way they have to leave the past and create a hopeful future.

That's the way it was for Mary McLeod Bethune. Born July 10, 1875, two years before the end of the Reconstruction (the time after the Civil War that slaves were given new lives), Mary and her family still lived in poverty.

When she was nine years old, Mary tagged along with her mother to take a basket of freshly washed and ironed clothes to her former master Ben Wilson's house. They had to go around the home to the entrance in the rear, the one through which the blacks could enter. In 1884 in Mayesville, South Carolina, there was absolute segregation between the races. Her mother went inside to take the family their clothes and receive the few cents paid for such a job.

Waiting outside, Mary was captivated by a children's playhouse and peeked inside. Two white girls about her age sat on scaled-down furniture. They were playing with their dolls.

"Hello, Mary! Do you want to come in?" one of them called out. Of course she did. Mary was just a little girl, and she wasn't admitted to such circles every day. A passion ignited in Mary that day. Seeing past her circumstances and limitations, she made a decision that changed her life and the lives of many after her.

You see, Mary was the fifteenth child of seventeen children. She was the first child born free to a family of former slaves. Her family only knew hard work, cotton fields, and difficult times. They were free and had five acres of land to work but nothing more. Mary wanted more, and this day made her determine how to go about it. She recounted the event in this manner:

> I picked up one of the books.... And one of the girls said to me—"You can't read that—put that down. I will show you some pictures over here," and when she said to me, "You can't read that—put that down," it just did something to my pride and to my heart that made me feel that someday I would read just as she was reading.

Mary McLeod Bethune discovered the world of education through that one act. She realized the plight of her race was limited by the lack of education, and she begged her parents for that opportunity. It came when the Mission Board of the Presbyterian Church sent one young black woman, Emma Wilson, in city clothes to educate the black children of South Carolina. Mary was the first to attend. She graduated from that school at age twelve, wanting more education but not having any way to achieve it. She prayed for a miracle.

A few years later Mary was awarded a scholarship that had been given by a Quaker woman in Colorado. She had a life savings she wanted to donate to allow one black child a chance to attend Scotia Seminary School in North Carolina. Mary became that child. After attending Scotia Seminary, she received a scholarship to the Moody Bible Institute in Chicago, where she continued to be a high achiever. Mary was the only African-American student there, and one of only a few non-whites.

But Mary didn't stop with her own education. After graduating from Moody Bible Institute, she moved to Daytona, Florida, where she began her own school in 1904: the Literary and Industrial School for Training Negro Girls. The beginnings were meager. Mary had only $1.50 to her name, five students, and shipping crates for desks. But she had a determined heart. Mary created opportunity through education for many that would not have received it anywhere else. She had immense faith in God, and believed that nothing was impossible. She remained president of the school for more than forty years.

Mary had only $1.50 to her name,
five students, and shipping crates for desks.
But she had a determined heart.

While much of her energy was devoted to keeping the College solvent, she also provided a better living condition for her parents and an education for her son and grandson. Two axioms of Mary's philosophy—"not for myself, but for others" and "I feel that as I give I get"—were confessed to Charles S. Johnson.

In 1954 she attended the World Assembly for Moral Re-Armament, an organization that subscribed to the principles Mary McLeod Bethune had lived by: "absolute honesty, absolute purity, absolute unselfishness, and absolute love."

For Mary, education was her tunnel to success. This is a story of the life education can create when it remains pure, teaching students to become better persons in every sense. Mary was taught academics, but as she became the teacher, she also taught love, faith, selflessness, and striving toward a better world.

Mary Bethune's education was practical for her time. Today we moms need to determine what is practical for our daughters. Our girls live in America where they drive cars, buy insurance, receive credit cards, apply for mortgages, get credit ratings, fill out applications, make resumes, cook food, file tax returns, and bring up children. Yet are these things being taught?

My younger daughter learned calculus to complete her fourth year of high school math for college entrance. I'll bet real money that's not the class she uses the most now that she's out on her own. Her sophomore year the school she attended offered an elective course on consumer math, educating students on auto insurance, credit ratings, bank reconciliation, mortgage rates, and more. I was insistent she take this because I knew it was a course she'd need for real life on her own. You cannot exist in America today without understanding credit, interest, insurance, banking, and many other daily tasks. Yet Algebra II, Calculus, and more are core classes—not consumer math.

Early in reviewing schools I was taken aback when meeting with one high school guidance counselor. I asked if a consumer math course was offered. He replied it was, but it really wasn't important for the student to take. Colleges would consider it an "easy class," and it wouldn't look good on my daughter's transcript.

I replied that it might not prepare her for college entrance, but it would prepare her for life—especially since she'd be spending many more years living in the real world than she would in college. He looked at me as if I didn't really get it, but I think he was the clueless one.

In days gone by, auto shop and home economics were offered. Should we not rethink those programs and any others that may be appropriate? We should add vocational schools and community college education and place it on the same level as other secondary institutions. There should not be any pomposity on behalf of the higher learning academic over practical learning. The offerings vocational schools and community colleges have are just as effective as the four-year institutions.

I'd love to see a professor of philosophy with a lofty attitude left without the local auto mechanic or dental hygienist. Broken-down cars and bad teeth would certainly get his attention. No one can philosophize his way off the side of the interstate when the car doesn't run. Perhaps in the absence of help when he was broken down, he'd begin to place appropriate value on these trades and treat them with the same respect and dignity he did his own course of studies.

*I'd love to see a professor of philosophy with a
lofty attitude left without the local auto
mechanic or dental hygienist.*

Above all, we need to reinstitute hope—hope for the future, integrated with faith. Yes, the *faith* word. To believe there is someone greater than we are and more competent shouldn't be that scary to most people. On the contrary, it should bring reassurance. Our country is so afraid of alienating the individual that they are denying the populace hope. Where are our children without it? This world is a difficult place to live, with hurt and heartache on every side. Our children are not shielded from it.

Teaching the principles Bethune had lived by—"absolute honesty, absolute purity, absolute unselfishness, and absolute love"—will offer hope where needed the most.

So here's the challenge the next time the school board and public officials state that the teachers are going to be cut because of a budget shortfall. Assemble your group of Academic Advocate mothers. Have the ones whose talents are research and numbers find the financial breakdown of the school system. Then allow the creative members of your group to take that information to create posters, charts, and presentation materials. The members of your group who love networking and public speaking can contact other mothers, local media, and address the school board.

What will this exercise prove? It's not the classroom that has the enormous amount of waste; it's the *administration*. That's where the spending cuts need to be placed. You will indeed expose some of the fallacy in their dialogue (and scare them a little into hopefully making the right choices for the sake of the children).

As Academic Advocates, let's take the words of Herbert Spencer, British philosopher and sociologist, to heart" "The great aim of education is not knowledge, but action." If we moms make a commitment to affect the school system of America, it *will be* changed, one school at a time—for our daughters and their daughters as well.

6

WANTED
Professor of Gender Studies

| Job Description |

Educator of the interdisciplinary study that explores the complex connections between the sexes, providing curriculum that explores and debates gender as one of the most fundamental facts of our existence. Must create in the student an understanding of the deep significance and the effect of political, economic, and social systems on the role of women in society.

Just in case you thought this mom job title was made up and doesn't exist in the real world, it's not and it does. This lofty, highbrow position is a real job at most universities. The course descriptions at these institutions sound somewhat vague and innocuous, but I can assure you the content isn't. Our universities as well as our culture are working overtime to tell young women who they are, what they should think about themselves, and what role in life their gender should play. The goal is to ultimately instill in them the conduct and nature of a female.

I can also assure you that this information has very little to do with your daughter's well-being and positive self-concept. There is another agenda actively at work. With throngs of "experts" intent on providing this instruction, you simply have to be the one who gets there first. *You* must be the first person to educate your daughter in Gender Studies, "providing curriculum that explores and debates gender as one of the most fundamental facts of our existence."

Simply said, your daughter needs to know how to live well and delight in the unique nature of being a female. She needs to understand the truth of "equality" in the genders and how to gracefully interact with the opposite sex. She must understand the good, the bad, and the ugly of female characteristics. So consider yourself officially enrolled in the curriculum required to obtain your doctorate in gender studies.

> *Your daughter needs to understand*
> *the truth of "equality" in the genders*
> *and how to gracefully interact*
> *with the opposite sex.*

Every doctorate degree requires time, research, and ends in a lengthy dissertation. For the mother version of this degree, life provides the time and the required research is personal observation of human nature. The mother's dissertation then comes orally—presented repeatedly to the audience and also to the absolute dismay of our very own daughters. What you do not need is a heady team of educators to perform a research project or a government grant to fund it; you simply need a bit of information and common sense.

This chapter will provide the information you'll need to support your position, as well as historical views with current analysis. But the conclusions most convincing are those made by observing the unique nature, grace, and strength of women who have lived before us. Those ladies simply by living understood how to be the women they were created to be.

A Grand Lady of Grit and Grace

Minnie Ethel Maness Brock, or better known by the family as "Minnie Mom," was my husband's paternal grandmother. This grand lady was made up of grit and grace. It was an honor to sit with her, gleaning vast amounts of wisdom. She was a Southern woman who lived most of her life in the mountains of Kentucky. Rearing eight children on very little money with a husband who worked on the railroad or at the sawmill, she raised everything they ate, sewed everything they wore, and worked harder than an American steel worker just to keep her family afloat.

When I met her, she was well into her seventies, with a completely white afro—the big, curly kind that sprouted in every direction. Minnie Mom was probably five-foot-seven and maybe 130 pounds. She was a little stooped, but mighty. The year the roofers worked on her home she would climb the ladder to join them. Whether it was because she thought they weren't doing the job the way she wanted or she was bringing them something to drink, we were unsure. It was probably both. Much to our dismay, this eighty-plus-year-old woman was on the roof.

What I was most in awe of was her wisdom. Minnie Mom's comments were always sage. She'd seen so much of life. When we visited with her in Kentucky following the birth of our second daughter, her advice to me was: "Two children are quite enough. God gave us two hands and two legs, so two is enough to handle."

Knowing she had many more than that, I asked, "But Minnie Mom, you had eight kids."

Her wry reply? "Yes, I did." With that simple statement she said everything she meant to say.

One of her most poignant stories came to me on a day that she and I were discussing politics during a presidential election year. Knowing her age, I asked her what year she began voting. Apparently, like most young women of her generation, she registered for this privilege soon after she got married. She joined the same party as her husband, whom I knew of as "Poppy" (he had passed away years prior), each year casting her vote in tandem with him…until the year of the "no account sheriff," that is.

> *"Two children are quite enough.*
> *God gave us two hands and two legs,*
> *so two is enough to handle."*
> —MINNIE MOM

This local election included a county sheriff she wasn't very sure about. Questioning her husband about this particular candidate, Minnie Mom found Poppy adamant. This sheriff was the representative of the party they belonged to and of course he would get their vote. So Minnie Ethel Brock voted as she always had with her husband.

Not long after the sheriff was elected, he was caught in shady deals. He accepted money he shouldn't have to do something he wasn't supposed to do. The constituents responded slowly but respond they did. When reelection came, he was resoundingly voted out of office. Even though her husband cast his vote straight party line, including for that sheriff, Minnie Mom broke ranks. As she put it, "Wasn't about to see that no-account sheriff in office anymore."

That was the year she vowed never again to vote for anyone because it was expected. When she told me that story with a sparkle in her eye, I believed that, for Minnie Brock, it was her Independence Day. This was not an act of rebellion or defiance; I never heard a word of disrespect or disparity toward her husband. Nothing really changed in their relationship. Her workload remained the same, and the struggles weren't any less. But Minnie Mom had insight about how to make independent decisions, and she became comfortable doing so. She grew as a woman in that year, adding acceptable independence to all her other life roles.

Changing Times

The year each of my daughters turned eighteen there was a presidential election. They could not have imagined anyone denying them their day in the voting booth. Yet, less than a hundred years ago, women were denied voting rights. That women would not have been allowed this privilege seems unbelievable. However, many historical rights previously denied to women in America have been won by strong, determined activists. Land ownership, legal rights, education, and that right to vote are only a few. These changes in their time were necessary but that was then and this is now.

Times have indeed changed. To prove that, let me give you a few statistics. In the year 2008, according to the National Science Foundation research, 62.3 percent of Associates Degrees, 57.3 percent of Bachelor degrees and 60.6 percent of Masters degrees were awarded to females. Based upon the Small Business Association's Office of Advocacy there were nearly 7.8 million women-owned businesses in the year 2007, generating 1.1 billion dollars in sales and doling out 218 million in annual payroll. In the 2008 Presidential election women had a higher voting rate (65.7 percent) than males (61.5 percent). In real numbers more women than men voted in both that election as well as the election in 2004.

The earnings ratio of women to men has seen annual increases from 1990 to date. While we may not have achieved equal pay for all positions, studies show that the current pay disparity is often accounted for by choice of careers and hours worked. I cite these statistics because you really need to know them. We as women have won our rights and have everything we need to succeed on the home front, in the workplace, in the political arena, with land ownership, and in so many areas. Then why are so many females still unhappy and dissatisfied?

The Subtle Costs of Feminism

Feminism, by definition, is the theory that men and women should be equal politically, economically, and socially. It's easy to agree with the basic philosophy of equality. Equality in genders is true and right. Even so, feminism has never held an allure for me. I have never felt inferior to a man, nor have I reared my daughters to feel inferior. By the same token, neither do I think a man should feel inferior to a woman. Equality is simply that we are on the same playing field of life—equal in talents and opportunity.

Equal—or superior?

But I'm convinced the platform of women's rights today doesn't care as much about *equal* rights as they are intent to achieve *superior* rights. Take time to research their current agendas, and you'll find they include abortion, liberalism, lesbianism, and independence from, as well as power over, men. Did you ever play "uncle" as a child? Sitting on top of a classmate, chiding her to cry "uncle" before you let her up? The women's rights movement is still sitting on top of their opponent. No matter how many "uncles" are screamed, they simply won't acknowledge they have won and move to let their opponents up.

*The platform of women's rights today doesn't care as much about **equal** rights as they are intent to achieve **superior** rights.*

In your research observe the generation of daughters that followed this age of the feminist. One of the early goals was to no longer be viewed as a sex object. The desire was for women to be respected and rewarded for their abilities, instead of being viewed through the prism of sex.

But what has transpired? Contrary to the stated goal, young ladies today have mastered the art of getting attention from their sexuality. The movement didn't change the power of sex or the innate ability for a young woman to understand and use that power. It simply failed to teach a daughter how to have an appropriate successful relationship with a man. The alternatives presented were to argue with, belittle, or manipulate our male counterparts. So when the next generation realized those alternatives didn't work well, they fell back to sex.

Identical—or different?

The second irony is that the movement created confusion. In attempting to be *equal,* we have mistakenly sought to be *identical.* By working for equal opportunities we have come to believe that we are equal in nature, ability, and desires. The wonderful part of the gender differences is that we are indeed different!

In 2003 the BBC News did a story entitled "What are the 78 differences between women and men?"[1] To get ideas flowing, four BBC participants added their thoughts, funny and enlightening:

> Women have the *if you need to be told, I'm not going to tell you* gene.
> —David Bergin Switzerland

> Men have a gene that enables them to maintain a vicelike grip on the remote control while reclining on the sofa studying the insides of the eyelids.
> —Jane, UK

> Men like to have all their stuff on show to impress their mates. Women like to hide things in cupboards.
> —Mark Nelson, UK

[1] 19 June, 2003; http://news.bbc.co.uk/2/hi/uk_news/3002946.stm

Women put things on the bottom stair to take up next time she has to go upstairs. Men just step over them until told to pick them up.
—Karen Kelsey, UK

Women can use sex to get what they want. Men cannot, as sex is what they want.
—Steve Munoz, US

These observations are endless, unscientific, and a testament to the fact that we don't need a government study or a doctorate to teach us we are different. We all get it. Live just a little bit of time relating with the opposite sex, and it becomes abundantly clear.

Then there's the science. "The New Sex Scorecard" in *Psychology Today* spoke of these physical and psychological differences. This study, while looking at the biology of male XY chromosomes versus the female XX chromosomes, went a little further and studied the gray matter of our brains. Did you know that women have 15 to 20 percent more gray matter—the ability for processing great amounts of information—than men? While men have larger brains than women, their brain mass has more white matter. White matter provides spatial reasoning, which is single-mindedness—the ability to focus and conquer life's tasks. Interestingly, white matter also is less easily damaged than gray matter.

These scientific facts boil down to this hypothetical scenario. Husband and wife are on a street corner in New York City. A mugger approaches. The wife, while seeing the cute red dress in the store window to her left, is impatiently waiting for the walk sign to illuminate, observing the family in the cab with the little boy wiggling anxiously, and simultaneously deciding what she will eat for dinner. The husband is concentrating on safely getting him and his wife back to the hotel to catch the end of the ball game.

Mugger approaches, husband immediately reacts to defend,

focused on stopping the event. Wife observes mugger's eye color and height, clings to purse, worries about husband, and wonders how the children will get along without them. Mugger hits man in the head, where he gets less damage than the wife would, knocks him down, and runs off with wife's purse. The wife is screaming every detail that just took place and searching for someone to call 911. As she bends down to care for her husband, she's still thinking about the children back home and wondering whether they'll make their dinner reservation.

The moral to this scenario is that these reactions and responses created by our nature are extremely complimentary. Taking our humanity back to the early years, a man can venture out into the forest and hunt more effectively and aggressively than a woman. One hour out in the woods without spotting dinner in moving form and most women would say, "Enough of that. I've got other things to do." But a woman can cook breakfast, dress for work, call the plumber, review homework, and bark orders to the children all at the same time.

One hour out in the woods without spotting dinner in moving form and most women would say, "Enough of that. I've got other things to do."

But using these examples doesn't mean I'm relegating women to these roles. Rather, I mean to show that we as women are *created to multitask*. A man is more instinctively the provider and family protector while the woman is the nurturer and caregiver.

And now my challenge to our feminist friends: Why is this a bad thing? While scientists are still debating what this means, there is undeniable evidence of the uniqueness of each gender. And those uniquenesses are amazing, exceptional, downright good things!

So let me ask you: assuming the women's movement achieved its goals of equality, which I believe in most instances it has, what now? Have these changes all been for our betterment?

Take a quick look at the realities. The relationship between the sexes, which was to be much improved by the movement, has disintegrated. Women may be getting paid better, but we are not necessarily treated better. The divorce rate is higher, domestic violence is rampant, and relationship commitments are absent. These are all indicators that the women's movement has failed. By accepting the premise that equal means identical, we have belittled the value of the men in a woman's life. We no longer need them. We believe we can do and be everything they can...and sometimes better.

> *By accepting the premise that equal means identical, we have belittled the value of the men in a woman's life.*

Professor friend, the truth is we cannot. By taking from a man a part of their very nature, we have left them feeling unfulfilled. A man wants and *needs* to be the protector and provider. They need to hunt the game, which translates, in our world today, to having a job that provides for the family. Their innermost desire is to be the defender of their wives and children. Keeping the family from harm's way is instinctual and part of every man's nature. A man needs to be the hero. Whether we women like to admit it or not, we love and need a hero too.

Women always need to be needed. When we are bettering someone else's life, we are happiest. Whether it is husband, children, coworker, parents, or friends, we feel fulfilled when we can help. That means the nature and the needs of men and women are complementary. The true way to achieve harmony in families is by embracing and respecting these differences. That's why a mother and a father in this complementary relationship provide the best instruction in their children's lives.

A few years ago I saw a very practical representation of the differences of gender. A television program had created a waiting room scenario, placing a hidden camera in the wall of the room. First, the mother and child were brought into that room. Then later, separately, the father and that same child entered the room. What happened next obliterated all conjecture on how the sexes would fill their time.

The mother entered, looked at the books on the table, and spoke softly to her child, discussing which book to read. Upon making that decision, the child crawled into the mother's lap, opened the book, and together they spent time reading each page. The children sat quietly, twisting their hair or sucking their thumbs, attentive to the stories in front of them. If they didn't go for the book, the mothers chose the puzzles on the coffee table. Turning the board upside down, the mother would assist her child in placing the pieces correctly into the spaces made. Each of these exercises ended with the mother simply holding her child in her lap and cuddling.

Later, the father and that same child would enter the waiting room. As they began their wait (supposedly for the study to start), they were usually sitting down. But invariably they got up from their seats to undertake some male form of entertainment. They hung the child upside down until she giggled to death, messing up her hair and disheveling her clothes. They walked the room, exploring, or even wrestled on the floor until both were tired. Not one time did the dads sit passively, awaiting their appointments.

Not a single father quietly read a book. Not a single mother became a pro-wrestler. Each parent fulfilled a need the child had that was unique to that parent's nature. Children become prepared for successful adulthood by growing up in an atmosphere of challenge and adventure from the father as well as comfort and caretaking from the mother.

Nurturing with No Regrets

In the question-and-answer section of your oral dissertation on the nature of a woman, ask your daughter this: When we live in a world of such need, why is it bad that we women are nurturers by nature?

Every day you will encounter the helpless, the homeless, and those who are sick, hurt, or injured. People are lonely; they need compassion, assistance, and love. We women have the unique ability to provide for much of this care. Make sure your daughter understands that nurturing is never a weak characteristic but an extremely strong one. When a woman recognizes a need and wants to help, she will move heaven and earth to make something happen. And when she does, the world changes!

A gender study has to include career choices—work both inside and outside of the home. The entire time my daughters were growing up I worked outside of the home. My husband and I became self-employed three months after we were married and built businesses together our entire married life. I never went without, at the very least, a full-time job.

When a woman recognizes a need
and wants to help, she will move heaven
and earth to make something happen.
And when she does, the world changes!

Evenings around the dinner table found our daughters often wearied by business discussions. They would beg, "Can we talk about something else?" We traveled a lot, taking them with us until school took over. When we lost control of their schedule, we made a commitment to set parenting as our top priority. Often we succeeded; sometimes we failed. Yet our daughters knew this: they were our treasure over anything else God had given us, and our commitment to them was without surrender.

I loved our work and felt it was an essential part of who I was. It helped me to grow and do things I never knew I could accomplish. The example set for our daughters in our business lives was that you could truly achieve anything.

But that example was not enough to help them become everything they could. And it was not enough for me to be successful at the office, either.

A personal telling moment came when some performers I was working with asked why I couldn't come to the airport and pick them up. They had flown in from a concert and needed a ride. I was having trouble working out their normal pickup and was about to surrender. Torn between my personal and corporate lives, I was overwhelmed by guilt feelings.

Then my moment of clarity came. My response was this: "When I am old and in the nursing home, I have only two people who may choose to visit me and wipe the drool from my chin. One is Chelsea and the other is Loren. I'm going home."

And so I did. All was not lost: the performers got a ride. I knew I had made the right decision. From that time on I chose to arrange my business life around my daughters every time I could. To this day, I have no regrets. I was fortunate enough to have both—life with my family and accomplishment in our business.

But not all mothers work outside of their homes, and my keen appreciation of the roles of stay-at-home moms came to me shortly after we were married.

One of my husband's college friends and his wife had invited us to stay with them when we were traveling through the town they lived in. I had never met either of them, so I was anxious to be liked.

We picked up my husband's friend at his office, where he rode with us to his home. Trying to make conversation, we talked of his family, his children...you know, small talk. Looking for a relatable platform, I asked the question often asked of a husband about his wife: "Does she work?"

His instant reply was this: "At the most difficult and important job in the world. She keeps our home and rears our children."

Boy, did I feel stupid. But he was right. We place so much value on jobs outside the home that we forget the most important role of a wife and mother. What could affect our world more than the molding of the generation that follows ours?

Our jobs in the home, outside of the home—whether just one, a little of each, or a lot of each—are all places we find ourselves in. Neither is the perfect or the only solution. What's important is that you find yourself on the path God made for you and that you don't judge those who are on different paths. I think we occasionally need to be reminded of the example set for us of the "noble wife" before we heap judgments on other women regarding their choices or wallow in guilt about our own.

The Proverbs 31 woman

To find an example of a woman who successfully performed her duties, there's no better place to look than the last chapter of Proverbs. (And no, we're not looking at her to make you feel guilty.)

The writer described her at length as "a wife of noble character." This title makes me wonder who she was. (If you think the term *wife* is condescending, throw that idea out right now. It comes from the foolishness taught in our university gender studies.) In today's world we assume this title placed a limit on her position and abilities. After all, we pride ourselves in being so much more than "just a wife." So how can the life of this woman, who lived so many years ago, relate to any demands we as women encounter today?

Read the story yourself sometime, and you'll realize nothing could be further from the truth. This woman was indeed a wife, yes, but she was so much more. Her husband sure seemed to like her a lot. In fact, the story says that, because of her, he looked really good to his friends. But that wasn't all she was. She was kind and loving, a humanitarian, a landowner, a businesswoman, a mother, a wife, an employer, and a teacher. Take a look for yourself: the virtuous women of Proverbs really held every one of those positions! Now how is *that* for a job description? (Some of you are feeling tired right now just thinking about it, aren't you?)

Speak of our overly committed, driven, obsessive women today, the Proverbs 31 woman had to have begun that parade. So, does this mean every one of us are supposed to be a teacher, landowner, businesswoman, wife, mother, and any other job someone can design for you. Well, no. Each mother is to apply the same premise of creative counseling they have already applied to their daughters to themselves. You mom should perform the duties and tasks that are unique to you, no more no less. So whether your life work keeps you on the home front or at another workplace, rest assured that the Proverbs 31 woman could indeed be a description of you.

> *Speak of our overly committed,*
> *driven, obsessive women today,*
> *the Proverbs 31 woman had to*
> *have begun that parade.*

It was just a few days ago that I had the pleasure of meeting another mom as we sat by one another in an airplane for a two-hour flight. As you do when confined to small spaces with hours to go, we began talking about our lives.

She was the mother of four grown daughters' I am the mother of two. She homeschooled her girls, I sent mine to public and private schools. She taught her daughters beauty was inside that they shouldn't dye their hair or feel the need to wear makeup. I dyed my daughter's hair pink in elementary school and shopped with them at the cosmetics counters. She stayed at home each day caring for her girls; I left for the office juggling the workplace with the home front. After recounting our unique histories we looked at each other and asked, "Well, how did it work out?" I am happy to report both of us replied, "Pretty good, we're proud of our girls." Then we went on to discuss their accomplishments. We had a wonderful conversation and really enjoyed one another's company.

I'm quite sure had we met when our girls were home in their growing-up years we'd probably have asked the obligatory questions. She may have responded she was a stay-at-home mom, and I would have responded I worked and traveled, raising my girls in the midst of my busy life. Then we both would have smiled, quickly pulled out our books; politely ignoring each other as soon as we found out we seemingly had nothing in common. I feel confident we would have been afraid of the remarks that often follow by many women when you state where you find yourself in life.

The conversation that goes something like this, "Oh, you don't stay home with your daughters, I see. Don't you miss out on a lot? I'm sure you'll find you can't be there when your daughter needs you? Where will she turn if you aren't?" Or "Didn't you go to school to be anything more than just a mom? I would think just being a stay at home mom would be so unfulfilling. Are you really happy with that decision? And truly don't you want your daughters to believe they can accomplish anything more in life than just housework and motherhood?"

The funny part is as we discussed our lives we both recounted those conversations. I was judged as the "working mom" by the stay at home moms. She was judged as the "stay at home" moms by the working moms. But now having grown daughters we know neither road is perfect, and neither road is always appropriate.

I wish I had known when my girls were growing up what I know now, we need each other, we need to support one another and we must never ever judge. Walking off that plane I reflected what different tracks she and I had taken and how amazing all six of our daughters were. Being a mom is hard enough without others telling you how you are doing it wrong. Remember: we only walk in our own shoes…no one else's. So forget those statements of judgment, get past the certainty that there is only one path and remember this job can be done well in many ways.

Gender nature ≠ gender talents

There's one last thing I have to add to this doctoral study. Never confuse gender nature with gender talents. We are equal as men and women, but predictable we are not. Because you are a female, you aren't automatically a better cook. Simply because you are male doesn't enable you to fix the toilet.

When Christmas comes in our family, the Dewalt drill under the tree is tagged MOM. I have received a drill, dremel, tool box, tool belt, and even a miter saw. These are gifts that traditionally are considered "men things." But I like fixing things. When we purchased our first home and were immensely poor, I figured out how to take a toilet down to the ground, fix all leaks, and put it back. We simply could not afford a plumber, and I had the brain for the task.

> *Because you are a female,*
> *you aren't automatically a better cook.*
> *Simply because you are male*
> *doesn't enable you to fix the toilet.*

My husband, on the other hand, was not blessed with mechanical reasoning. He stares at anything that needs to be repaired with a look of bewilderment. The talents given him are of the broad strokes: he is a visionary, a marketer. He has always been the one who dreams big and achieves goals other people don't think can be done. He is an information hound who makes wonderful decisions on everything from building a record company to marketing whatever project we are currently involved in and buying or selling just about anything. He leads the parade; I take care of the details. And this partnership has been the anchor of his and my lives through the best and worst of days.

So, Professor Mom, examine the cultural representation of gender offered to your daughters. Then observe the lives led to complete that Professorship of Gender Studies degree. Take the time to study and understand this subject. But, most of all, embrace this. Recognize your own worth, your unique nature, and your distinct abilities. If we earn that doctorate for our own betterment and then incorporate it in our lives, our daughters will most likely do the same.

Recognize your own worth, your unique nature, and your distinct abilities.

If your daughter wants to take the gender studies class at her college of choice, make sure she has her head intact before she jumps in. She must understand fully what a woman and man's true nature is. I can assure you those truths will run contrary to much of what is being taught in that class. Sadly, if she disagrees with the teacher's academic premise, she may be treated only slightly better than the resident lab rats.

Since so much is packed in this gender studies role, here's a quick review:

- Women were denied equal rights but are no longer. Statistics prove that we have all the opportunities we desire to pursue.

• Science proves that genders are indeed different. Life proves what those differences are—and how delightful and complementary they can be.

• Our actions dictate our relationship with the opposite sex. Manipulating through sex has only a short-term effect; arguing and belittling tears a man down. If we respect and recognize the worth of a man's nature, they will treasure ours.

• Finally, it is not where you work—whether inside the home, outside the home, or a little or a lot of both—that determines your success as a woman. It is embracing your nature as a woman and placing your priorities in what really matters.

So now Professor, begin the oral recitation to your audience—in this case, your daughter—and make sure you continue it until you no longer have breath.

Funny thing is, if you do, in a few short years you'll find her reciting the same things to *her* daughter...and someday to her daughter's daughter.

Now that's an enduring legacy you can be proud of.

7

WANTED
Relationship Counselor

| Job Description |

Provider of counseling to develop the ability to recognize, avoid, manage, or reconcile troublesome differences in relationships. Through instruction, as well as information, instill within the counselee the knowledge needed to build and maintain a successful bond that ends in mutually enriched relationships.

Your daughter arrives home from a date. She's simply beside herself when she comes to your room to tell you about it.

"I'm in love," she says. "He's the cutest, sweetest, most precious thing you've ever seen." Her heart pounds when he's around. She loves to be seen with this young man. He makes her laugh, buys her presents, and says the most brilliant things. Etc., etc., etc., the accolades go on. Believable of any human they are not, but she thinks they are entirely true. In her eyes, this gentleman walks on water.

You, on this night, are fortunate, because she's reporting all of her crazy emotions to you.

The first time this scenario happens, she's a young teen. His name is implanted on notebook paper in never-ending doodles. The giggles are boundless when she's on the telephone with her friends, and the terror upon seeing signs that he may like someone else is intense.

From your life perspective, you know this "love" is usually short-lived. This wonderful boy will lead to another terrific guy. She'll discover that he is not the love of her life, and that he's not perfect, either. (It will take her even longer to discover that neither is she.) Indeed, something will change in that "amazing" relationship and she will move on.

But if you say as much now to your precious girl, this "true love" might indeed last longer than you'd prefer it would just to prove you wrong. Keeping your mouth shut and smiling numbly is, without a doubt, your best defense. Remember: he is only *today's* Mr. Right. There are more to come.

Life predicts there will likely be a day when your daughter comes home with that look in her eye, telling you a certain someone is her one and only, the perfect man, *and on that day she will mean it.* Maybe he's not a great guy. With your age and experience, you know things she doesn't. Human nature seen at twenty years old isn't as clear as that seen at forty years old. So there's a chance that you know what's behind the flowers given and the sweet things said. You might also have a good guess that this young man will not be the faithful partner you'd want for your daughter. He doesn't possess what's needed to be half of a strong relationship.

Remember: he is only *today's* Mr. Right. There are more to come.

What should you do now? You are on dangerous and slippery terrain, and your responsibility as a mother is way behind the curve for these sorts of conversations. That's why it's so important that you *do not wait* until that day to instill the traits that make good and enduring life relationships.

The "Laundry List"

An effective Relationship Counselor spends years prior to that moment helping your counselee know what a good man is and what it takes to build a great marriage. This job has to begin early because when your daughter falls in love, she really FALLS in love. At this moment in your daughter's life you can quickly become the enemy—the person who "understands nothing" and needs to be avoided at all cost. If she isn't looking for the right relationship prior to this moment, she can land squarely in love with the wrong one. And there's nothing you can do then to steer her away.

Loren and Chelsea still recite my laundry list for "the man they should marry." My relationship counseling began when my daughters were very young and thought boys had cooties. Then I repeated it to them when they entered middle school. Those were the days they liked a scrawny boy who was caught somewhere between Little League and cars.

My relationship counseling began
when my daughters were very young
and thought boys had cooties.

For the lovestruck growing-up girl, the highs and lows are huge. Your knowledge of her heartbreak might only come when you walk slowly by your daughter's bedroom door and stop to pick fuzz off the carpet. (In fact, it's such an unbelievable amount of fuzz that it takes quite some time to collect.) It's then you "accidentally" overhear your daughter speaking to her best friend about her agony. Gaining knowledge you can't let out that you know, you discreetly, yet effectively, use that information in your ongoing counseling process.

High school was no different for my daughters. So I again pulled out my Relationship Counselor card. Each time a boy came to the house I nonchalantly mentioned my laundry list a short while later. The list was simple:

1. He pays his bills.
2. He loves his mother.
3. He loves God.
4. He loves you.

The list seemed silly to my daughters at the time. I got a lot of the rolling eyes, the "Oh Mom!" and the silence that said, "I am not listening," but to this day, Chelsea and Loren can still recite it verbatim.

Financial integrity

You see, there was a method to my counseling madness. Successful or unsuccessful relationships are built upon the character of the participants, and certain barometers reveal that character. If a young man can pay his bills, he usually fulfills his commitments. There is a good chance integrity and honesty matter to him. If he can be forthright in his financial obligations, he won't carelessly get his family in debt, nor will he back down from his obligation to his family. He'll take the helm of provision seriously and fulfill it well.

Of course, such barometers are not foolproof, but they are great indicators for your daughter to gauge the integrity of the man she plans to spend the rest of her life with. I believe the "equal rights movement" and instant gratification culture has created a great gulf in this character trait in men. Many young men today have been raised to believe financial responsibility isn't important and not required. Both males and females have not been taught financial restraint. So, at the very least, if this young man is not good at bill paying but great at everything else, then your daughter had better be good at it. And he must agree to hand the checkbook

111

over willingly, leaving the begging for possessions behind.

Financial integrity—the ability to keep one's financial commitments—is also one of the most obvious indicators on how capable a person is to keep all commitments. This includes the commitment to the very relationship your daughter is building.

Conduct toward his mother

A young woman should always look at how her boyfriend treats his mother. All Relationship Counselors understand that his conduct toward his mother is an amazing insight into his respect for and ability to love a woman.

Conversations between the young man and his mom are previews of the dialogues your daughter can expect to have with her spouse. He must be able to talk about both the important and the mundane. Females do both. But, if we women are honest, we'll admit we truly excel in the mundane. We can ramble on about *every* detail of *every* event. Most men hit the high spots and move on. They're good with that, even if it leaves us longing for more.

Finding a compromise for these opposing communication styles is, and will be, trying. Starting out on the right foot in a relationship is crucial.

No relationship problem can be solved or any understanding of issues reached unless a man makes the time to listen to what sounds to him like babble. At the same time, a woman must learn when she should simply shut up. That man can't and should not be expected to listen to each and every word spoken. (So leave the longer version for your chats with your girlfriends who want you to tell all.)

If this boy has the ability to communicate with his mother *with respect* about the important and the mundane, he's well ahead of the game.

If a son and mother love each other well, your daughter has a running start toward a rich, rewarding bond—not to mention the potential of a warm, mutual relationship with her mother-in-law, who is also then likely to treat her, as a new member of their family, with respect.

His love for God

As you and your daughter are considering that "spouse for life," never forget that in every person there is some root faith. This even includes faith in the fact that there is no God in which to base your faith. Faith is the belief in something where there is no concrete proof. Believing there is no God isn't proven any more easily scientifically than the faith that there is a God. Sharing your root belief system is imperative to sharing a future. I am grateful my daughters' belief in God is an anchor for them and a source for their life decisions. Finding a spouse who shares that faith is not only ideal but, must always be nonnegotiable.

If consulting and relying on a spiritual authority is part of your daughter's decision-making process, it will be impossible for her to have a lifelong mate who doesn't feel that faith is vital to their daily life as a couple. This, of course, is based on the presupposition that marriage is intended to last until death takes a life partner. So the plan is, when you marry, *this* is the person you're going to grow old with.

Imagine spending the next fifty-plus years not talking about or acting upon your faith. A couple shares a home, a car, a bed, and children but can't share their faith? It simply doesn't work. A Relationship Counselor must emphasize that sharing *all things* is crucial in a marriage bond—most of all, your faith. Why is this so important? Because our faith is the deepest part of our soul, and without sharing that depth, the marriage will most likely fail.

Imagine spending the next fifty-plus years not talking about or acting upon your faith.

113

His love for you

There's a reason I put financial integrity, his conduct toward his mother, and his love for God as the first three items on my laundry list, and I put "loves you" last. Most people believe "loves you" should be in first position. But it's not the most important.

(Right now some of you just dropped your jaw and you're frowning. But hear me out first. Then you can decide for yourself if I'm off-base or not.)

Love is needed, desired, and a delightful element in all relationships. But love as it is currently viewed by our society is emotional, and emotion has great days and bad days. Its roller-coaster nature cannot be relied upon as a fix for the challenges that come as a result of daily life.

Love is truly wonderful and important, but as an emotion it is not enough for success in building strong relationships. Love warms the heart, earns trust and confidence, and cares for others. But love's fickle nature can't be the only place to start a life. If it was, every boy—heart pounding and palms sweating—your daughter brought home would automatically attain the position of spouse. (Now there's a scary thought, isn't it?)

No, it's when *love* becomes a verb—an action word—that it is most effective. Love as an emotion is not enough, but love, when acted upon, becomes rich, rewarding, and successful.

*It's when **love** becomes a verb—an action word—that it is most effective.*

Back to Basics: The Kindergarten Rules

To create the basis for success in relationships, there is another duty for the Relationship Counselor. This important duty you will teach all throughout their lives, but the irony is that it really comes from their early years. You see, kindergarten is the time to learn what makes a marriage successful.

Kindergarten Rules are great relationship counseling tools, and they include these:

- Use an indoor voice.
- Listen when others are speaking.
- Treat others with kindness.
- Be honest and truthful.
- Share with your classmates.

Teaching your daughter these basic life rules and making sure she adheres to them is the foundation of any good relationship. If the Kindergarten Rules are used at every stage in life, all relationships will be improved. But the marriage partnership will benefit the most.

A successful wife and husband are not "made" on the Wedding Day. In fact, that beautiful, exciting event that is all about them as a couple has no relevance on whether there even is a "them" twenty-five years later. What they have learned as the principle rules for the treatment of others is the cornerstone of all relationships, and this is especially true for their treatment of their future spouse.

Somewhere in the late 1990s, as my husband and I worked in our office, I heard guffawing, excited comments, and the normal noise a group of tickled women can make. As I entered the conference room, I found these precious twenty-somethings eating lunch together. They were some of the brightest, most talented, fun, and delightful women you could ever meet. They worked extremely hard in every area and position of our business. We could not have succeeded without their efforts; they were truly the best of the best.

What had them so entertained? They had found an article supposedly from a 1950s home economics book. The publication was well before their years of education, and upon taking a peek I knew there was no way it would be part of the current education curriculum. Totally politically incorrect, this text would create a major uprising. But because I simply can't resist a good time, I joined the group.

What they were reading was intended for high school girls, to teach them how to prepare for married life.

What to Do When Your Husband Comes Home

• Have dinner ready: Plan ahead, even the night before, to have a delicious meal—on time. This is a way of letting him know that you have been thinking about him and are concerned about his needs. Most men are hungry when they come home and the prospect of a good meal is part of the warm welcome needed.

• Prepare yourself: Take 15 minutes to rest so you will be refreshed when he arrives. Touch up your makeup, put a ribbon in your hair, and be fresh looking. He has just been with a lot of work-weary people. Be a little gay and a little more interesting. His boring day may need a lift.

• Clear away the clutter. Make one last trip through the house just before your husband arrives, gathering up schoolbooks, toys, paper, etc. Then run a dust cloth over the tables. Your husband will feel he has reached a haven of rest and order, and it will give you a lift too.

• Prepare the children: Take a few minutes to wash the children's hands and faces if they are small, comb their hair, and if necessary, change their clothes. They are little treasures, and he would like to see them playing the part.

• Minimize the noise: At the time of his arrival, eliminate all noise of washer, dryer, dishwasher, or vacuum. Try to encourage the children to be quiet. Greet him with a warm smile and be glad to see him.

• Some don'ts: Don't greet him with problems or complaints. Don't complain if he's late for dinner. Count this as minor compared with what he might have gone through that day.

• Make him comfortable: Have him lean back in a comfortable chair or suggest that he lie down in the bedroom. Have a cool or warm drink ready for him. Arrange his pillow and offer to take off his shoes. Speak in a low, soft, soothing, and pleasant voice. Allow him to relax and unwind.

• Listen to him: You may have a dozen things to tell him but the moment of his arrival is not the time. Let him talk first.

• Make the evening his: Never complain if he does not take you out to dinner or to other places of entertainment; instead try to understand his world of strain and pressure, his need to be home and relax.

• The goal: Try to make your home a place of peace and order where your husband can relax.

No wonder my colleagues were amused. This article contained Stepford wife material—a view of a seemingly brainless, unimportant human created solely to fulfill her husband's needs. There also was no evidence that the counterpart instructions were written in any shop class textbook for the high school male student to prepare him for marriage.

So that day in the conference room we laughed in incredulity that any woman would be that crazy—or that "submissive"—to do those things.

Then, when the laughter died and I walked away, it suddenly hit me as I headed up the stairs, back to my office: what if we women did just a *few* of those things for our men? Yes, times are different today. Many of us are in the workplace as well as keeping up with the home front. That means both parents arrive home tired from their day. Both need the quiet home of peace and order. But if we want that special home, why don't we women step up to the plate and begin doing some little things that would go a long way in our man's heart?

I thought of the girls in the conference room. They were in various stages of relationships. It was a season when some had sworn off men after being hurt, others were in the casual dating phase, a few were in serious relationships or engaged, a couple had already married, and some were already divorced. Yet to all of them, the list seemed absurd.

So the next day I asked a few of them a question: "What would happen if you chose only *two* of the things on the list to do...and then you acted upon them with a serious face!"

Of course, some of the items on the 1950s list are unrealistic, but the premise behind the list isn't. So I said, "Why not try it? And see what happens?"

I believed then and believe now that every woman would be amazed at how doing those two little things would affect how they were treated by the men in their life in return.

Why not take the challenge yourself? It isn't ridiculous to do something for your spouse to make his or her life better. It takes a strong woman, not a weak one, to commit to caring for another human for the rest of her life. And truly men today are so used to being treated as anything but special that they notice and love it when you show extra kindness and understanding.

And here's the reward for you: If your man is the kind who has the qualities for lasting marriage, and you chose him wisely, he'll do the same for you.

The Jewels in Your Treasure Box

Here's a lasting relationship tip: Kindness breeds kindness. It promotes emotional health. A relationship with two people caring for one another's needs takes the emotion of love to an entirely new level of action.

It's as if when you were first married, your love was that of a small diamond. Building a life together takes that treasure and yearly adds jewels. In the end, your love becomes more of a treasure chest than a single diamond. It is filled with all your "together" moments as you've faced financial struggle, financial success, your daughter's birth, and your daughter's rebellion. You've experienced the death of family members, cars breaking down, shopping for your first home, and loading the car for your daughter's first trip to college. Each of these life events, when experienced and handled together, adds an additional jewel to that chest that can never be taken from a committed marriage.

My daughters cannot truly understand what over thirty years of marriage means to the depth of my husband's and my relationship, because they have not experienced such a relationship yet. Nor can I understand the loss my father-in-law experienced when my mother-in-law died after forty-plus years of marriage. Half of who he is…is now gone. A life partner is truly someone to be cared for and treated as a precious jewel. This is love in action. His or her worth is priceless. We need one another.

A life partner is truly someone to be cared for and treated as a precious jewel.

Your daughter needs a partner as well. Preparing her to be successful in this role is tantamount to her training.

In one episode of the old television program *Dr. Quinn, Medicine Woman,* a dialogue was going on between the shopkeeper and Dr. Quinn's youngest son. The two were lost in the woods together. The boy, then thirteen, was extremely confused and needed a man to discuss issues of his age. The issues, of course, were girls, sex, and how he should feel about the whole subject. Listening attentively, the shopkeeper pondered for a while before he made this statement: "A man needs a woman for one thing...." Of course, the show went to a commercial at that moment.

What is the one thing we all believe that men need women for? Sex, of course. I thought with dismay, *Surely the shopkeeper isn't going to be that simple. The writers have to do better than that.*

After awaiting the commercial break, the scene returned. The shopkeeper looked at the young boy and finished his statement: "...to believe in him."

I smiled. The writers certainly got that one right. A man can do anything if the woman he loves believes in him. A woman can do anything if the man she loves respects, cares for, and protects her.

Until death do us part?

I can't walk away from the subject of relationships without acknowledging where we find ourselves regarding the permanency of marriage: believing that marriage is intended to last until "death do us part"; that the promise made when you marry should never be treated lightly. The assurance you make to your future spouse on that wedding day should always be a promise you mean to keep. Yet current statistics tell us that nearly 50 percent of marriages in America will end in divorce.

So how do we maneuver through this new frontier? A great spouse and a fulfilling relationship is your hope, your dream for your girl, and for your own life. But I also know that you or your daughter may find you have entered an unexpected path. Choosing the wrong marriage partner can lead to anything but marital bliss.

Your daughter might have memorized that laundry list. She might be able to quote it to you backwards and forwards. But the day may come when she inexplicably believes the list really isn't relevant—at least not with *this* young man who is "close enough." Or she falls for someone who, on the surface, displays all of the character traits she is looking for...that is, until he becomes her spouse. You will probably see the truth before that time, but she doesn't.

Well, Mom, what do you do? Before she gets to that planned wedding day, when you know in your heart the relationship could be a mistake, you will discuss, cajole, and challenge, hoping to change her mind. You will lead them toward an effective premarital counselor to expose any future minefields. You will remind her of the list, look at the character of this future spouse, doing your best to get her off this course.

When you know in your heart
the relationship could be a mistake,
you will discuss, cajole, and challenge,
hoping to change her mind.

But, sometimes, you just can't. This may be the one time she will not listen. Her heart is leading her decisions; her head is not. It is then you must love like you never have before, offering unlimited mercy and grace. She's got a rough road ahead.

If that happens, you must remain in her life and help her make this marriage work. Here's where you must have the grit (as well as the grace). Support this young couple. Listen and assist

121

when you find tools that might make their marriage change course. Speak when you should; step out when you shouldn't. And above all, never give up hope.

But no matter what you or she does, the day may come when you receive that tearful call. The call to tell you she can't do it anymore and has determined to end the marriage (or her husband has). I can tell you this because I received that call and realized this needed to be my time of grace. My elder daughter needed me just like your daughter, if facing this, will need you. The pain she experiences as a result of her unwise decision will be deep and difficult.

What I have learned about divorce is that it is a profound loss, one that creates grief, bereavement, and heartache, no matter what the cause. This is a loss of something that should have been, a loss of young dreams, heartfelt desires, and honorable intentions. You must love your daughter through the grief and the healing.

But it's not only your *daughter* who can face this challenge. You may find *yourself* as one of those "statistics"—a woman who is facing or has faced divorce. It's a situation you never thought you'd be in, and now you too must confront the same loss and disappointment. Mom, extend grace to yourself as well. Healing is offered and available to you in the same way it is your daughter. For the sake of your family and your future, you must embrace that healing and accept that grace, believing it is there for you. Without it, you won't be able to move forward in life with the grit that's required in such circumstances.

Mom, if you find yourself in that place of divorce, there's also one more difficult thing you need to do that your divorcing daughter may not. You must show grace toward the father of your girl. As her father, he holds a vital position in her life. She needs him, so it's incredibly important that you do your best to help her hold onto and build that relationship. Your words and actions will be one of the greatest determinants in achieving this goal.

None of us wants to join the disheartening statistics count of divorce. That's why, if your girl is facing an enormous marital challenge, you must fight alongside her with all your might to help her build that healthy commitment. Help her if she can save that seemingly impossible relationship, transforming a marriage that would otherwise end. Help her make it to that "twenty-five years later" treasure chest that enriches her and her husband's life. Mom, she needs you more now than ever.

Abigail Adams: love and understanding

Abigail Adams (the wife of John Adams, the second President of the United States) is a pure representation of the richness of marriage. This fascinating woman was strong, courageous, and often left alone while her husband followed his career path. While he was away, she successfully managed the family farm. During the Revolutionary War, she singlehandedly cared for their family while John defended the life he wanted for his country.

A man can do anything
if the woman he loves believes in him.

Their marriage lasted fifty-four years, yet many troubled days they were uncertain if they would both remain in this world. Life at these times was precarious at best, since multiple people were out to kill the Patriot John Quincy Adams.

Abigail was known for her letters, spelling out the struggles through those trials. One such letter, dated October 16, 1774 and written just prior to the outbreak of war with Great Britain, told of her great relationship with John, her support and belief in what he did, and her emotional commitment to him:

I dare not express to you at three hundred miles' distance, how ardently I long for your return…. And whether the end will be tragical Heaven only knows. You cannot be, I know, nor do I wish to see you, an inactive spectator; but if the sword be drawn, I bid adieu to all domestic felicity, and look forward to that country where there are neither wars nor rumors of war, in the firm belief that through the mercy of its King we shall both rejoice there together.

Your most affectionate
Abigail Adams

Knowing John was a man who had to fight for what he believed in, Abigail found herself in fear for his death. The real possibility of his demise lay heavy upon her heart. She believed her peaceful life would end, and she wouldn't regain happiness until they could once again meet in the "country where there are neither wars nor rumors of wars."

A woman can do anything if the man she loves respects, cares for, and protects her.

That kind of deep love and understanding between husband and wife is what most only aspire to, yet that is exactly the kind of love we need to teach our daughters to bring to a marriage. The Relationship Counseling pinnacle is an agreement made by both partners—an unselfish commitment to the betterment of the one they pledge their lives to. If you teach them that love is a verb when they are young, and they heed your instruction by seeking an equal partner with the same goals, it is a love that can be achieved.

8

WANTED
Sex Ed Teacher

| Job Description |

Provide direct instruction to students regarding human sexual anatomy, sexual reproduction, sexual intercourse, reproductive health, emotional relations, reproductive rights and responsibilities, and other aspects of human sexual behavior. Carry out a wide variety of tasks in the teaching-learning process for students—the primary one being to help students learn the subject matter and gain the understanding that will contribute to their development as mature, able, and responsible adults.

D o we really have to do this job? I mean, really? Certainly there are plenty of educational opportunities on human sexuality ready to instruct your daughter. They come in the form of books, teachers, sex-ed classrooms, television shows, the internet, movies, and even your daughter's friends. But it's this well-laid-out minefield of misinformation and agenda that makes it crucial this instruction is YOURS to give. The fact the rest of the world is clamoring to meet this need pinpoints how vital this job is for a mom.

Is it easy? No, not when your goal is to provide clarity with appropriate insights. But keep in mind that others who want to inform your child of the "facts" may have goals that aren't even in the same ball park as yours.

Even the most open and forthright mom has issues with this job. After all, your sweet little girl is asking questions that require an enormous amount of frankness. You'd rather she forget this subject for one more year and go back outside to play. *She's so young to talk about this,* you think.

You'd rather she forget this subject for one more year and go back outside to play.

But let me ask you: where else would you rather she go to get this kind of information? Can you think of a single better source than you, the one person who cares only about your daughter's well-being? You have no other motive but the self-interest of your girl; indeed you are the best person for this job.

So I made a commitment early on to answer any question when asked—without hesitation or embarrassment and honestly and appropriately. There was nothing I would leave unanswered. Simply ask, and I'd respond. I was determined to beat the other educators to the punch in a timely and well-thought-out approach.

It was a great plan, and it pretty much worked until the day my twelve-year-old daughter asked how homosexuals had sex. I hadn't seen that one coming, and I swallowed hard. But then I stoically put on my game face. I asked her repeatedly if she was *absolutely sure* she wanted to know. When she'd responded, "I wouldn't have asked if I didn't" with eyes rolling no less than four times, I inhaled deeply and jumped in.

To this day she still remembers that conversation unbelievably well. And let me tell you: so do I. Her face mirrored every thought that could be measured on this subject in the twelve-year-old mind. Her reactions were loud and, at times, humorous and priceless. My face and reactions were working overtime to stay impassively intact. The education was honest, factually correct, and without editorial. I'm not sure how well she slept that night, but she was educated.

You may think that conversation is not appropriate to have with a twelve-year-old. Well, maybe it's not, but my daughter was curious about it. If I hadn't answered, she would have sought answers from someone else. I knew what I would teach her about this subject but I didn't know what that someone else would say. Would she then have been educated with the truth, if she talked with someone who had an agenda to pass on?

So, Mom, you are now a Sex Ed Teacher—whether you are comfortable with it or not. The good news is that while this job does require those "human sexuality" talks, a successful Sex Education comes from so much more than just biology.

By placing an enormous amount of importance on that one birds-and-the-bees conversation, we mothers miss the target. There are many entities that feel sex education is their domain. And they believe they do it extremely well. Sexual education is gained from school, television, peers, and organizations structured to teach this subject. It is thoroughly explored and explosively divisive. All of our community wants to educate our children on sexuality. They pride themselves in their understanding of the issue. But if that education is so successful, why have we not changed the landscape of sexual confusion and consequence?

Girls are getting pregnant at a higher rate than generations before us, even though there is an abundance of birth-control options. Venereal diseases are at an all-time high. Sexually deviant behavior is rampant, so perhaps public school education or media presentation of sexuality isn't "the solution." The ability to handle this issue does not come from any one educational program or influence. To face sexual issues a girl must draw upon an entirely different value platform: the confidence in her value, in her own worth. This comes from the love and nurturing of a family, that supportive belief system in each and every girl.

Confidence in her self-worth is the only foundation that will enable a young lady to live in, and get through, a sexually drenched culture relatively unscathed. That means before being confronted with these issues, a girl must first believe in herself. A healthy, balanced view of herself *must* precede her knowledge of how she is viewed.

The Middle-School Years

The middle-school years are my least favorite years of life. They are the hardest, most emotionally agonizing times in the course of growing up. At least it seems that way to both mother and daughter when you are in the middle of them. Having already gone through those years with my two girls, I received a telephone call from a dear friend one Tuesday afternoon. She was on her way to the car pool line in front of her daughter's middle school, and she was clearly distressed. I could hear the dismay in her voice and sensed the angst in her heart. Her daughter was the recipient of the "mean girl" attack. We all know that one: girl against girl with the end purpose being the superiority of one over the inferiority of the other.

Her precious, independent daughter was the object of the "you're weird, stupid, not cool, etc." remarks. And they hurt. Worse, the daughter had just entered a new middle school and was seeking to find her place. She was simply being who she'd always been and, apparently for certain middle-school peers, that wasn't acceptable.

For those of you who don't yet know, middle school isn't culturally about being you; it's about being like every other middle-school clone simply to fit in. The audacity of this girl to be an independent thinker was anathema to the middle-school elite. And the daggers of ridicule rained upon this sweet child.

I believe it hurt my friend, like most of us mothers, as much or more than it injured her daughter. What to do? Call the teacher, the other girl's parent, fight back, kick the girl in the car pool line, ignore her, or something else? This was the debate. Ever seen a lion cub being defended by their mother? At this moment a mother makes the lioness look lightweight.

Middle school isn't culturally about being you; it's about being like every other middle-school clone simply to fit in.

When my daughters were subjected to this rite of passage, my creativity was brilliant, if I do say so myself. Imagine the scene with me:

Me, the mother, comes to the defense of my bullied daughter. Wheeling into the school parking lot, horn blazing, tires squealing, I stop traffic and leap out of my SUV to confront the mean girl who is making my daughter miserable. Everyone stands aside, stricken into silence, as I stride forward until I am toe-to-toe with Middle School Diva. What do I tell her?

"Back off. If you even as much as look at my daughter the wrong way, you will deal with me. And by the way, if you don't know 'Miss Smug Little Think I'm All That,' you are simply a blip on the screen of humanity. The only place in life you will feel important is here and now, and trust me, it will soon be gone."

The crowd around me, evidently as sick of Miss Diva as I am, cheers and applauds. My daughter looks at me in awe as her hero.

I load up the car and head home, problem solved....

Okay, so I didn't do it. It wouldn't have worked. My daughter would have been mortified, dying of embarrassment instead of bullying.

But I must say that dreaming it at the time felt good...*really good.* Yet when I calmed down, I realized they were simply the insane fantasies of an out-of-control lioness defending her cub. My basic instinct was to defend, fight, and make the wrong right. But what was really needed was my ability to maintain my reason and sanity…and then do what was best for my daughters.

Girls need to understand that middle school is only the *beginning* of a series of these conflicts. Throughout their years on this earth, your daughter will encounter people who feel the need to rebalance the playing field of life. They will be requesting things of your daughter that are not in her best interest. These people will do their best to manipulate their point of view into the mind of your girl. That's because they must feel superior to, advance beyond, and even sometimes simply be mean to the people around them. Sad to say, many of these individuals don't outgrow the middle-school scene; they practice it in daily life even as adults.

So this is the perfect opportunity to teach your daughter practical self-worth. My friend's girl had been reared to be an independent thinker—to follow her own special path based upon a specific value system. She had a healthy dose of self-worth already instilled. Did that mean the bullying didn't hurt? Of course not. But the nurturing given by her parents for her first twelve years now was faced with a life test.

This is the moment for effective Sex Education—not the "sex talk" but the "how to live independently among those who want to bring you and/or your gender down" talk.

I said to my troubled friend, "Tell your daughter this: life is full of people who have different opinions than yours. A lot of them will be uncomfortable with the fact that you won't agree. Instead of accepting an independent thinker, they choose to attack, thinking they can cause you to relent and become 'one of the pack.' These people find it unacceptable that a confident free thinker stands unaffected in their midst. They need to feel important and in charge so the verbal assault you're getting is to make them feel superior. They must make others conform to their attitudes to create that self-importance in themselves.

"A child who doesn't follow the path of these personalities is an obstacle to them. So if you are simply yourself, and you feel good about yourself the way you are, they have nowhere to go and nothing left to ridicule. They have lost their effectiveness. That's the one thing that will truly drive these girls out of their minds."

This is one of the important life lessons your daughter needs to learn early and well.

It doesn't mean your daughter, as the recipient of the attack, won't feel hurt or alone; she will. But if your daughter learns in middle school that attacks are based upon the attacker's need or desire, rather than your daughter's own inadequacy, she'll be way down the road in dealing with other life pressures. She'll be able to face opponents with a different attitude, an understanding of why it's happening, and her self-worth will stay intact.

> *Attacks are based upon the attacker's need or desire, rather than your daughter's own inadequacy.*

So, Mom, don't do anything in your current middle-school crisis...at least not to anyone else and not yet. Talk to your daughter; remind her how special and unique she is. Educate her so she understands this form of confrontation. Let your daughter know that this is the beginning of people trying to influence her actions. For as long as she has her own independent personality and makes her own decisions, these people will come in and out of her life. But she doesn't need to allow them to control her.

The one thing you must do as a communicator is to make sure she is talking. As long as she is sharing such struggles with you, she'll be all right because you can lend perspective and also keep a keen eye on the situation. Indeed, if it gets worse and you are seeing it take a permanent toll on your child's self-worth, you must find a way to intervene. But don't jump in if they are just dealing with the fallout. It's permanent damage you're looking for. Know that hurt and recovery create strength. So if your daughter can get through this situation with her independence and self-worth intact, she has passed an important test for a successful future.

Putting Sex in Its Place

Right now you're wondering, *Mmm, sounds like good advice, but what does all that have to do with sex?*

Self-worth has absolutely everything to do with it. Sex is powerful and one of the most manipulated subjects in our culture. Simplified, every boy is a walking hormone; every girl innately understands the power of sex.

At eight years of age a little girl giggles and flirts; then a little boy chases and pulls her ponytail. At the same time they both yell at each other, "Cooties!" This is the elementary school mating dance. Middle school is full of confused relationships; high school begins the courtship in earnest.

Every boy is a walking hormone;
every girl innately understands
the power of sex.

A girl must believe that she is created for much more than the physical gratification of someone else. That knowledge will temper the influence sexual pressure can place upon her life.

I often wonder where we got the idea that our children have absolutely no self-control. We speak of them as if they are no more than animals in mating season. We act as if they are unable to *not* have sex, so we've lowered our expectations: "When you're ready and with the right person, practice safe sex," the diatribe goes. But what are we really saying? Early and uncontrollable sex is a given for our daughters. Nowhere in the majority of sexual education is there the "Hey, it might be a great idea *not* to have sex" plan.

No disease, no unwanted pregnancy, no lowering of self-esteem, and no regrets are a few of the benefits of virginity. As in all other aspects of life, do we not want the absolute best for our daughters?

Modern sex education tries to dupe us into thinking that times have changed, and there are no consequences to that change in attitude toward the sexual experience. The facts don't bear that out. A survey of teens 15-17 years of age was done by the Kaiser Foundation in partnership with *Seventeen* magazine. These findings show that 76 percent of girls and 55 percent of boys regretted having sex. In a second survey done by *Seventeen* magazine and the Ms. Foundation a thousand 13-21 year olds were surveyed; 81 percent of the girls and 60 percent of the boys regretted the decision to become sexually active. Interestingly, these studies were not done by any organization that actively promotes abstinence.

Each year over three million teens contract sexually transmitted infections (STIs and STDs). That's one out of every four teens who is sexually active. The human papilloma virus is an STI that causes genital warts and also is the cause of 90 percent of diagnosed cervical cancer in later years. So we think vaccination for this is a good idea...but what about all of the other consequences of teen sex? HPV is also the current number-one cause of oral cancer. The acceptance of casual oral sex has created an outbreak that outpaces smoking in this horrific, deadly illness.

It is proven that a much higher rate of contracting chlamydia, an inflammatory disease of the pelvis, in found in teen girls. This STD has a significantly increased rate of future infertility for teenage girls than the women that contract this disease at an older age. Stunningly all STDs are sexist in nature; they statistically do more serious physical damage to women than men. In other words, it's our girls who will be hurt the most.

The rate of depression among teenage girls having sex is 25.3 percent while the rate among teens not having sex is 7.7 percent. Attempted suicide rate among girls having sex is 14.3 percent compared to those who maintain abstinence at 5.1 percent.

With these facts, exactly why are we perceived as ill-informed and unrealistic when we know abstinence is in our girls' best interest? Protecting your child from regret, depression, emotional issues, and physical problems, including cancer that can lead to death, seems a no-brainer—the right thing to do. It would seem a teacher in any subject would want to teach principles of success. So why should Sex Ed be any different?

All STDs are sexist in nature.

The study of those who came before us has always fascinated me. Headstones marking the graves of lives that have been lived give little information on their hopes and dreams. If you walk from site to site, you may find family members, a baby who died at birth, and a child who was outlived years by her mother. Epitaphs read of family love, heartbreak with the loss of a child, and the noble who died battling for our freedom. There is so much to be discovered about the people who walked this earth before us.

Yet as you learn history, there is something largely unwritten: the subject of sex. Sex did not appear to have a great part in human life, at least not in the recorded version. Textbooks didn't contain volumes of information on the matter. Neither were there written journals, how-to books, or scientific exploration of the subject.

But knowing history, we have to know that sex was a part of life; each generation begat the next generation. After all, this unspoken irony enables us to have continuing human history. It doesn't take an educator to know that without sex there would be no next generation. There was only one recording of the Immaculate Conception; everyone else is conceived the same way.

So in the importance of our world history, sex ranks incredibly low. Understanding that humans achieved much in the past *without* a sex educator leads me to ask: Why now does this subject hold such a prominent place in our culture? I truly believe there is a concerted effort to destroy in this world, and I don't think the people involved in this effort even understand that is the end of their education. Statistics consistently prove the destructive nature of sex outside the confines of marriage in an objective debate. And it doesn't even take statistics to convince us. When our daughters or our friend's daughters buy into the lies presented to them, we see the damage firsthand.

While you are educating on this subject, don't forget to explain the pleasure of sex as well. "What?" you're saying. "Why would I do that?"

It may seem that downplaying sexual enjoyment would dissuade your daughter from having sex, so taking away the upside to the subject seems a decent plan. Well, it's not. If we act as if sex cannot be fun, we are not being truthful. There is pleasure found in any healthy sexual relationship. Yes, physical pleasure can be found in inappropriately timed sex as well, at least for a season. If you are honest in your education, which must be your commitment (otherwise your daughter will go to other sources for the information), you must give the complete, unabridged version.

"Sex can be fun anytime—pushing the right buttons, so to speak," you tell your daughter. "But it is only fully and completely pleasurable, emotionally and physically, and without damaging side effects in the marriage relationship with your life partner."

Controlling Sex...Before It Controls You

The most wise man who ever lived was King Solomon. Though known for his wealth, his proverbs had a lot to say about relationships. It is amazing to me that a man who married 700 women and had 300 concubines was considered the wisest man who ever lived. Having a gaggle of women under one roof, with you as the only man, isn't the most brilliant thing Solomon ever did. In fact, it seems like lunacy! But it does appear that early in the king's life he understood the depth and commitment of love. He wrote of love, passion, and sexuality in the Song of Songs—a book about a relationship between a man and woman.

This story is transcribed as a narrative by the lover, beloved, and friends of the lovers. It's a beautiful portrait of what a love commitment should be. The lover and beloved are entering marriage having waited for each other sexually and now will share their lives in every way. There is one statement repeated by the object of his love, his wife to be. In speaking to fellow maidens about her love and passion for this man she shares wise instruction with her peers: "Do not arouse or awaken love before it so desires."

Understanding that there is a time to arouse and awaken love, she warns that doing so prematurely serves an injustice to a future relationship of sharing and commitment. The natural act of love is sex. But remember that *love* and *sex* are not automatically synonymous. They are and always will be *separate acts* entwined well only in a marriage, with our life partner.

In a culture that creates the impression we as humans are slaves to the power of sex, how do you not arouse love? How do you not take that next step? The current thought is we are incapable of controlling sex; it controls us. So do we believe the theory that "Teens are incapable of keeping their pants zipped, so just make sure they are protected"? No, young women can choose to stay out of the back seat. They have been able to in the past. But they must understand the practical side of how to do it.

For years my daughters' lullaby was Stevie Wonder's "Isn't She Lovely?"—our love song to our girls. It's still a very special song in our family. But when they became older, I added a new song to the family musical repertoire. "(Don't you) Feel My Leg" was a song performed by Maria Muldaur when I was in my late teen years. It's a very useful tool in the education you are trying to achieve. The lyrics go like this:

Don't you feel my leg, don't you feel my leg cause when you feel my leg you're going to feel my thigh and if you feel my thigh you're going to tell a lie so don't you feel my leg.

Don't you drink that wine, don't you drink that wine, cause when you drink that wine you'll try and change my mind and if you change my mind you'll feel my fine behind, so don't you feel my leg.

You said you'd take me out like a gentleman—treat me fine, though I know that's just something at the back of your mind. If you keep drinking oh you're going to get fresh and you'll wind up begging for this fine, fine flesh.

Don't you feel my leg, don't you feel my leg cause when you feel my leg your gonna feel my thigh, and if you feel my thigh you gonna go up high, so don't you feel my leg.[2]

No, it isn't a sweet lullaby, but it's practical and full of truth, isn't it? Be willing to set Sweet Mommy aside when you tackle this job of Sex Ed. Use whatever tool necessary, including the wonderful ditty I just shared with you. Any mother who thinks she must be delicate about this subject is fooling herself.

A girl doesn't wake up one morning and say to herself, *I think I'll have sex today.* This, like everything else, happens gradually. Kisses lead to cuddling, which leads to hands, which leads to clothing unbuttoning, which leads to oral sex, which then ends up as ultimately full-on, no-stopping-the-train sex. And we all know this doesn't happen in one night.

A girl doesn't wake up one morning and say to herself, I think I'll have sex today.

Instruct your daughters that each act leads to another act. Decisions to not have sex are not made on a date; they're made at

[2] 14 December, 2010, http://www.moron.nl/lyrics.php?id=36043&artist= Big%20Bad%20Voodoo%20Daddy.

home—*before* the boyfriends, the dating, the automobile rides, the dances, or any other teen experience.

In Sex Ed your daughter will receive the sex talk, the biology version that begins with scientific facts, to the "don't do it" line, and that talk will end with "see you in a few years." But don't stop there; educate your girl to understand action and reaction from her and the boy...*any* boy. Prepare her, train her, educate her. Use whatever example is needed to paint the picture for your girl.

- If there's no gas in the car, it won't run. (A classic line my daughters thought was stupid.)
- He won't buy the cow if the milk is for free. (A truth from Minnie Mom).
- "Don't you feel my leg cause..." (Make sure they know the rest of the song.)

Get Creative

One of my best friends had a creative approach when her daughter once purchased her own bikini made up of a few well-placed hearts. My friend told her daughter it was inappropriate, bringing attention where she really shouldn't have it. This attention would only create problems for her and any boy who wasn't blind. She got the "Mom you're wrong! It does not, and you don't understand. And I'm not taking it back, either!" response as her daughter stomped away into her room and slammed the door.

Frustrated with her seeming inability to get across truth to her daughter, this creative mother tried another approach.

The family always had pets, and this year they had a cute little house dog. Taking scissors, construction paper, and tape the mother went to work. Cutting out three hearts and creating two-sided tape she stuck the hearts on the belly side of the dog in the same places they would be on her daughter.

Then she called her family into the room. Holding the front paws of the dog up, with the hearts dominating the scene, she paraded the dog around the room on his back feet while singing "Itsy Bitsy Teeny Weeny Yellow Polka Dot Bikini." After the family got off the floor from laughing, they revisited the conversation.

"Where exactly did you look when you first saw the dog?" the mom asked.

There was no denial, but an admission that eyes were no longer drawn to the cute little snout or puppy dog eyes, but elsewhere. Her girl couldn't argue with that. The mom's point was made and accepted; the suit was returned to the store. Who needs another lecture? Why not be original in your presentation?

Sexuality is powerful, and girls know it. Boys' heads turn when skin is shown, when girls dress provocatively. That's the simple part to figure out. The challenge is interpreting what is "too much skin." Yet doing so is an important role for us mothers as we battle the sexual behavior frontier.

Appearance is really important to most girls. They want to wear the current clothes, be cute, fit in, and inevitably this creates the forever wide divide between generations. Can they have uniquely dyed hair (probably), pierced eyebrows (maybe), short skirts (well, define "short")? Style can be displayed for your daughter in many ways. Help her find the style that enables her to feel good about herself, while at the same time not presenting herself as a person willing to do something she doesn't want to do.

As you approach this mountaintop of conflict in style versus modesty, I have three suggestions.

#1: Don't engage.

During my clothing struggle years with my own daughters a wise woman gave me great advice. When your daughter reaches thirteen, she's in the dressing room, and she says, "Mom, what do you think?" you never—I mean *never*—give the straight answer. Saying "You are absolutely crazy if you think that you are going out in public, let alone out of this dressing room wearing that! That's gonna happen over my dead body" isn't exactly the recipe for success.

Instead, being the wise mother you've become, your response should always be, "I'm not sure, honey. What do you think?"

Then she'll respond with her own uncertain comments, since at that age she is almost always uncertain about everything. Quickly you have your exit strategy from a potential catastrophe. Acknowledge her doubt and create a discussion about color, print, or any innocuous, nonthreatening aspect of her garment. This will end with you being able to say, "You are so pretty we have to find something that makes that shine. This just isn't good enough."

Your response should always be, "I'm not sure, honey. What do you think?"

This type of conversation is so much better than the alternative one that ends with the defiant "Mom didn't like it, so I'm buying it and wearing it to church!"

Without a doubt, this technique works. I've used it a million times myself with both my daughters—and avoided at least that many struggles. When not in the department store struggles, a mother should find time for further conversation when there are no other potential emotional bombs ready to go off. As you're in the car singing oldies together, or watching TV, comment on some cute but fashionable outfit that you think your daughter would look great in. Believe me, she'll pick up on it.

#2: Wage war on what matters long-term.

Your daughter needs to know that, in every part of life, half of a battle is won before she ever gets to war. In business, when the one you are negotiating with thinks you are a great negotiator, you'll get a better deal before you even start the process. In entertainment, if you look like a celebrity, you are perceived as one well before success enters your life. In the real battlefield of war, if you look like the stronger army, the enemy thinks they have a good chance of losing, so hesitancy on their part leads to your victory.

It's the same in sexuality. When a girl is dressed like she's ready to play, she'll be asked to play. The best way to avoid that assumption on the part of the boy is to not look like you think you were made for entertainment. Now, I'm not talking turtlenecks and corduroy pants that are a size too big; I'm talking about effective compromises. Never forget your daughter has to survive in the teen culture, so let style be incorporated in her world. For example, the day my daughter wanted pink hair, I didn't have a problem with it. It wasn't a battle that mattered. However, neckline to belly button *is* the war that needs to be waged.

Protect them, prepare them, support them, believe in them, and choose your battles: this is all part of effective sex education. Our daughters don't have to fall slave to current philosophies. Every daughter should know that no girl was created to simply be the object of another's sexual gratification. She was not brought into this world to be viewed as nothing more than a sexual partner.

When it comes to sex, "the first time" philosophy comes to our girls defined in many ways. What is the appropriate first time? When you're in love, he's amazingly cute, or the full moon is out? Clarity on this position requires definition on the part of the mother.

I look back to when my daughter took her first airplane trip by herself, to visit her grandparents on her own when she was nine years of age. She spent part of her homecoming day with me at my office. She loved wandering around our staff desks and talking to the wonderful people who worked for us. That day I got distracted with work and lost her in the building.

While rounding a corner as I searched for her, I heard her going from desk to desk, proudly telling people she took her first airplane trip all by herself. I stayed hidden as I listened to the responses that inevitably included stories of each person's first plane-ride memory. It struck me that day that a first in life only happens once. It can't be rewound and done again. It's over and is a memory. So find your own story, your own example to teach your daughter that there is only one first.

A first in life only happens once.
It can't be rewound and done again.

With sex, that first memory should always be good. Yet, because of our culture's standards, often it is not. Your girl should define that first with the man she intends to spend the rest of her life with after she marries. Such an experience will forever make that first special. That day will come without regrets, bringing no other relationships into that moment, and allow them to experience the wonder of sex in the most precious, fulfilling way.

#3: Realize you will both make mistakes.

I can't end this chapter without making you keenly aware of something. You will, at times, make mistakes in this career of motherhood. Know that your daughter will also make life mistakes, and sex leads the way during the teen and young-adult years. In this subject of sex will be the largest amount of confusion, conflict, and pressure for your daughter.

Don't be surprised if your daughter steps over lines she never meant to. There is, in fact, a good chance she will. But your role as Sex Ed Teacher doesn't end if your daughter steps past holding hands and kissing into more dangerous territory. It doesn't end even if she loses her virginity.

If any of those challenges are in your life right now, make sure you live in a way that shows an enormous amount of grace. Show grace to other moms, other daughters, friends, and family members who are dealing with consequences of choices in this arena filled with minefields. If you have shown that grace, there is a chance your daughter will believe she will receive the same. She will share her struggles with you and ask for your advice. Your relationship as mom and daughter will become stronger-than-ever because she now realizes that, in at least this area, your words were right.

Has she disappointed you? Yes. Are you wondering what you did wrong? Yes. Do you wish you could rewind life's clock? Absolutely, yes! But you can't, and your daughter needs you now more than ever. What she is working through currently is not the abstract but the concrete: real-life consequences.

Don't be surprised if your daughter steps over lines she never meant to.

She may have guilt, confusion, and regrets, have an STI, or even have become pregnant. Don't let her down now. Sex Ed Teacher, your job is even more crucial in these moments. The support you give her, the grace you extend to her, and the insight you can provide will help determine how much long-term damage there will be.

So Mom, love your daughter now in the same way you loved her the first day you met. Remember that day? You knew then there would be no mountain too high, no river too wide, no battle too great. Did you really mean what you said and thought that day?

I bet you did. And now's the time she'll know you did.

9

Wanted
Financial Consultant

| Job Description |

Supply financial solutions to client, educating them on means
of improvement of their financial decisions. Provide the
assistance needed to meet financial goals through personalized,
in-depth counseling and recommendations of appropriate
money management.

For years I was the "end cap" queen of America. An end cap,
for those of you who don't know, is the shelf space at the
end of each aisle in almost every store in our nation. It's the
"this is an unbelievable deal" vortex that pulls in busy women
when they are shopping in a hurry. It's the place where retailers
place the coolest stuff at the best prices. Really, can these buys be
resisted? Not by me, at least for a time in my life. I mean, can we
live without a portable chopper that works off batteries, cutting
everything instantly into the appropriate-sized pieces? But get it
home and find out what a nightmare it is to clean after shredding
all of your food instead of that promised "clean chop."

Or the cute little top that was only $6.99…and still lies in the
bottom of your drawer. (It doesn't match a thing you own.)

Seeking one lost shoe on the floor of my daughter's closet

would require weeding through the pile of must-have toys or undone projects purchased on a whim.

In hindsight, I wonder how much money I've spent on "stuff." I don't think I really want to know; it would probably make me ill. Back then I was vulnerable, in a hurry, drawn into the eddy of great deals. My jobs kept me running, while taking care of my family, our home, and our dog. I was merely trying to stay afloat without sinking. I was the perfect mark for advertisers.

I wonder how much money I've spent on "stuff."

I don't say this to excuse my bad habits; what I did still wasn't brilliant financial planning. But I fell, almost nonthinking, into easy spending...until it occurred to me that retailers were winning the game. Yet, even more than retailers beating me, I realized my actions were the most effective teacher, and I was instructing my daughters as a Financial Consultant too. What were my daughters learning from me? That a quick, mindless purchase was okay.

One of my jobs as Mom was to teach financial responsibility, and I certainly wasn't practicing it. So how could I expect them to?

The Financial Consultant's job is to understand money, to know what importance it holds, and how to manage it. So Mom, this job begins in *your own* life. You don't have to be an accountant to do this well. Just know how much you earn, don't spend more than you make, and don't purchase things you don't need. Never waste what you've been given. If you are expecting schools to teach this to your child, dream on. Remember from your Academic Advocate position that they care about algebra and calculus, not consumer math. The job is yours: to help your daughter learn how to survive financially in this money-driven culture. It's okay if math is not your thing; what you need to teach are financial limits and a balanced, healthy perspective.

The Allure of Money and Things

I have been bewildered at the broadly held belief that money holds answers and eliminates all life problems. The year that a game show posed the question "Who Wants to Be a Millionaire?" the resounding answer of "I DO" came from all corners of America. Of course that's not saying that a million dollars (in truth, around $600,000 after taxes), wouldn't help pay some bills; it would. But what money doesn't do is remove all hurt, solve life difficulties, and guarantee happiness.

While waiting at an elevator in LA with my daughter, who was going to see a doctor, we were joined by an obviously wealthy and extremely old woman. She was in a wheelchair pushed by a private nurse. Dressed impeccably, with a vast amount of valuable jewels on her hands and around her neck, she appeared unbelievably frail. But she barked unkind orders to her nurse, as if unhappy with everything around her.

As she boarded the elevator with us, I could only think, *Well, her wealth certainly didn't make her happy.* She was obviously very ill, toward the end of her life, unhappy, and accompanied by a nurse, instead of a loved one. She was a living example of wealth not bringing with it all that really matters.

The "I wants"

Don't think your daughter is safe from the deceptive allure of things. The phrase "I want" permeates the world around us. She will be taught at a very early age that possessions are extremely important. The first time you turn on the television to view a children's program she is inundated with commercials that sell her the best new toy. Beautiful little girls playing happily with the newest offering at the local toy store ensure that your daughter will want one too.

The phrase "I want"
permeates the world around us.

All through her life she will be presented with a new "got to have" item. Whether it is toys, cereal, shoes, makeup, new fashions, a computer, an electronic game, or the latest cell phone, these alluring items come fast and hard at your daughter each and every day. Remember, of course, that each product is inescapably linked to happiness, beauty, and life fulfillment!

If you don't get drawn into this black hole of buying the latest and greatest, you will indeed help your daughter avoid it. Now I'm not saying each and every purchase is wrong and that we should all live communally without possessions. I lived that way for a while and, trust me, it has its own pitfalls. What I am telling you is that you must have a *reason* to make purchases.

When I transitioned from end-cap mania to control over my purchases, I began a new philosophy of spur-of-the-moment buying for my daughters. Instead of buying whatever was offered, we began the tradition of buying a purposeful, not holiday-related gift. Occasionally I would purchase what we called an "I love you" present. These were special items not based on a day or event. They were not bought because someone in the shopping cart was whining over the "must have" they spotted. Or because I couldn't walk by the most amazing, well-priced item on the end cap.

These items were purchased because I loved my daughters. I wanted to show them a simple, non-pressured way to receive gifts. I did this occasionally, not every time we entered a store. And when I did, it was a special gift at a special moment for no reason other than I loved them. That was a great reason to make a purchase. They and I treasured those gifts more than any related to a life event.

Money—evil or good?

Even while you are training your daughters as well as yourself how to appropriately spend money, there is another view held by many. This outlook is interchangeable and dogmatic, depending upon the financial position you're viewing it from.

The first is that money is evil and those who have it did something wrong to get it. This view normally comes from one who doesn't have it.

Others think that possessing money proves worth and importance. This thought comes from one who does.

Then there are those that think poverty is a deficiency on the part of those who struggle.

Or the antithesis of that thought is that poverty is noble.

What I know to be true is that money and possessions, or the lack thereof, are neither good nor bad. The state of lacking is not noble, nor is state of having evil. It is what you do with the position given that determines your success in life. Your daughter needs to know that well.

If a child is born into wealth what do they do with that opportunity? If a child is born into poverty how do they achieve from that platform? Then finally, no matter what the economic state of your family is in financial instruction teaches your child how to manage money not let money manage them. There are a couple of lives I find fascinating that I believe exemplify this well.

Florence Nightingale

Named after the city she was born in—Florence, Italy—Florence Nightingale lived her life in England. Her inspiration crossed oceans and ignited change within the community of nursing in the entire world.

She was reared in enormous affluence and wealth, an extremely educated young woman. Florence's mother was so enamored with social life when launching her daughters into society that she added six bedrooms to their home to accommodate the entertaining she desired. The two Nightingale daughters were cared for by maids, footmen, and valets; they traveled between two mansions in England. There was nothing Florence either needed or desired that was not provided for her easily, elaborately, and with no consideration of the cost.

However, though Florence traveled with all economic opportunity, she found herself fascinated by social questions of the day and felt called to a different life: "I craved for some regular occupation, for something worth doing, instead of frittering time away on useless trifles."

Such urgings began her exploration of the societal needs of her community, where she visited the homes of the sick. Her discovery of the quandary these people found themselves in led her to seek an answer to their substandard care. She found that the means of change came through the position of nursing.

As her peers attended balls, flirting with young men while sporting new dresses, Florence desired more. The life she sought was providing the care for those who were ill. In the early 1800s the career of nursing was a common one, not respected by affluence. It was performed by poor women who had no other option. Her family, thinking it beneath this young lady of affluence and position, would not support her desire.

Relentless in her purpose, she spent the next fourteen years consistently persuading her family to support her in pursuing this career. She didn't want to defy her parents, yet she could not deny her passion. Finally, with their blessing, she began in a position at the Institution for the Care of Sick Gentlewomen in Distressed Circumstances—simply a poor hospital for women. It was there she began her road of social reform. Florence was trained as a nurse while on the job with absolutely no pay from this hospital.

It was in 1844 that she launched her crusade to change the conditions of hospitals after having worked in unbearable circumstances. She found hospitals in squalor with the nursing profession nothing short of low-level maids and determined to singlehandedly reform these institutions.

The real impact was made when she headed the nursing unit during the Crimean War. Not even wanted by the doctors at these British medical facilities, she was appointed to oversee female nurses in the military hospitals in Turkey. She arrived with a party of thirty-eight nurses and began the difficult and thankless duty of assisting the physicians and caring for the needs of the wounded.

The conditions they found of filth and inefficiency caused the mortality rate of the soldiers to be seven times higher in the hospital than on the battlefield. Miss Nightingale set about to change these by assisting both in effectively receiving incoming supplies as well as efficiency of care at the hospital. To accomplish this, she used the family relationships and acquaintances she had made while traveling as a young woman. When the war was over and the nurses sent home, Miss Nightingale personally saw to the financial needs of each nurse, paying them out of her own pocket.

As a result of her lifelong struggles with politicians and medical authorities, there was unprecedented reform. Florence used the money subscribed to her name after the Crimean War not for herself but to found the Nightingale Home for Nurses. She was the first woman ever to receive the Order of Merit. Nursing as a profession and sanitary conditions in hospitals were forever changed by Florence Nightingale's life.

Nursing as a profession
and sanitary conditions in hospitals
were forever changed by
Florence Nightingale's life.

Understandably, her life evokes feelings of admiration and respect. But if we look deeply into her specific achievements, we'd find that she probably wouldn't have been able to accomplish such dramatic change if she hadn't been born into wealth. She wouldn't have been able to work without pay while training to be a nurse. She'd have been unable to assist her fellow nurses financially at the end of the Crimean War.

There is also a real chance that she wouldn't have been socially prepared to approach political influencers effectively had she not been world traveled. In other words, Florence would have lacked the connections with those same people to seek and gain an audience that enabled her to garner much-needed supplies. She also used printed news to elicit public support—something she would have understood only as a result of her education.

It is from a life of wealth that Florence Nightingale achieved such high results. So is it wrong to have money? No. It is the way in which wealth is viewed and used that can create problems or be the means to solutions.

So make sure you tell your daughter that it's not wrong to have money. Mothers, this may very well be the place in life you find your family. If so, teach your daughter how to manage that financial position. It is not something to be proud of or ashamed of. Nor should it be depended upon, since having money holds no real security. It can be here one day, and gone the next.

Money truly cannot buy the things that matter in life. But it can be used as a launching pad for accomplishments that couldn't be achieved without financial opportunity. Remember, having money at your daughter's disposal becomes purposeless if she only learns to love the wealth she was born with and not to respect what she can accomplish with it.

Money truly cannot buy the things that matter in life. But it can be used as a launching pad for accomplishments that couldn't be achieved without financial opportunity.

151

Johanna (Anne) Sullivan

It isn't only wealth that is often considered indicative of what your daughter can become; it is also those born into poverty. This is never to be taught as a determinant of personal success. Poverty doesn't make life decisions for your child any more than wealth does.

Much has been written about the blind and deaf Helen Keller, but it is her teacher, Anne Sullivan, who I find most interesting. The success she achieved in the life of this handicapped child was inspiration for the untapped potential of many who were considered less capable because of their physical shortcomings. Reading the story of *The Miracle Worker,* one wonders where the strength and determination of this teacher was shaped.

Johanna (Anne) Sullivan was born in Feeding Hills, Massachusetts in 1866 to Irish immigrants. Unfortunately this family was less than ideal. Her father, an abusive alcoholic, left his children when Anne was a mere ten years of age.

But even before that heartbreaking blow, she suffered a life filled with heartache. Her only brother, Jimmie, was crippled by tuberculosis near birth. At age five Anne was struck with trachoma, leaving her almost blind. Then at age eight she lost her mother, who died of pneumonia. Their living conditions were those of abject poverty.

Abandoning Anne and her brother to relatives, and then the state "poorhouse" in Tewksbury, Massachusetts, Anne's father permanently left his parental responsibility behind. This institution was for charity cases, including the mentally ill, prostitutes, and those incapable of functioning in society. Left with only her brother, Anne was dealt one final family blow. Jimmie died shortly after their arrival at Tewksbury. Anne was truly alone.

The poorhouse had no formal educational program, yet Anne was insistent to learn. Her chance came when Frank Sanborn, chairman of the state board of charities, visited the institution where Anne lived. She followed on his heels relentlessly as he toured the facility, begging for the opportunity to go to the school for the blind.

As Mr. Sanborn ended his investigation of the facility at the end of the day, he exited with Anne still pleading to go to school. Not long afterwards, she learned she was to be sent to the Perkins Institute for the Blind. Her persistence had succeeded in Mr. Sanborn acting on her behalf.

Entering the school at age fourteen, unable to read or write and willful from years of neglect, she fought to fit in, often rebelling and struggling with the structure of the school and her peers. As Anne wrote:

I know that gradually I began to accept things as they were, and rebel less and less. The realization came to me that I could not alter anything but myself. I must accept the conventional order of society if I were to succeed at anything. I must bend to the inevitable, and govern my life by experience, not by might-have-beens.

With that disposition, at age twenty she graduated valedictorian of her class. Only six years prior she had begun her education without even elementary abilities, yet in the end Anne was triumphant. Through surgeries during her stay at the Perkins Institute for the Blind, Anne's eyesight was regained.

*I could not alter anything
but myself.*
—ANNE SULLIVAN

Prepared with this sight, her education, and a will to succeed, she took the position as teacher with the Keller family. And in that job she accomplished the legendary story in the life of Helen Keller: against all odds, Anne Sullivan taught a blind and deaf child how to communicate with the world.

It was not only poverty that Anne Sullivan was born into; she had many more struggles to overcome than financial ones. But her story is a motivating one to show that being without is not an excuse to not pursue life success. Poverty does not determine what any daughter can accomplish, and we should not allow it to be portrayed that it does.

If Miss Sullivan had had an easy life, would she have been steeled enough for the battle before her? I think her life is exactly what prepared her for greatness. Financial, physical, or emotional difficulty is not a negative in life; it can be used to shape your daughter's strength of character.

My prayer is that no little girl would ever have to suffer what Anne Sullivan did. That no child would ever experience the heartache she felt. But if life falls that way for your daughter, may she discover what Anne Sullivan learned: "I must bend to the inevitable, and govern my life by experience, not by might-have-beens." Then she can choose Anne Sullivan's path and accomplish more than any less harsh circumstance would ever allow!

Living In-Between

Being rich or poor is not often the issue. Most of us lie somewhere in-between. As a Financial Counselor, you must make sure your daughter learns how to manage money and that mismanagement doesn't destroy her. Many young women find, to their shock, that money is controlling their lives; they are not in control of money. Has your daughter begun receiving credit card applications yet? If not, they will soon come. In fact, many colleges in our country allow credit-card companies solicitation access to their students, for a fee. An eighteen-year-old who's clueless about financial management but holds credit cards that will allow her to spend $3,000 without any means of paying it off is a scary thing indeed.

What's even scarier is that, at eighteen years of age, your daughter can sign an application from the credit card company—or several companies—and suddenly have a billfold of cards at her disposal without you ever knowing. In America today it's nearly a rite of passage for our daughters, by their early twenties, to get a credit card and charge to the limit.

So let me make you a little more nervous. According to Sallie Mae, the leading national provider of higher education student loans, college undergraduates carry an average credit card balance of $3,173. With 18 percent interest making a $75 a month payment, it would take over sixteen years for that card to be paid off. Even more eye-opening is the fact that seniors graduate with a four-year degree and an *average* credit-card debt of $4,100—*in addition to* their accumulated student loans.

So, how do you counsel and plan through this minefield? After all, your daughter is of age and credit-card companies will be after her, offering her an easy way to take care of the "I wants." All she has to do, in fact, is fill out an extremely short application.

O great Financial Counselor, that's why it's so important to teach them about money when they are young!

Because my husband and I worked in our own businesses, our vacations were some of the most precious times we had with our daughters. They were often the only times we completely got away from the demands of work and concentrated solely on our family. Every one of the Brocks looked forward to them.

When it came to vacations, I believed that family memories were imperative, so I was determined to create many. No matter the personal cost, I was committed to the fun.

The year my girls asked me to do a headstand in the pool of the condo we were staying in, I foolishly agreed. I was easily forty years of age and looked out of my mind with my feet kicking in the air and head underwater. I'm sure I provided an enormous amount of entertainment for the sunbathers poolside who thought, *What on earth is that woman doing?*

It took me at least three attempts to get a hand on the bottom of the pool. I could only use one hand because I was holding my nose with the other. The first two attempts I flailed like I was drowning, but the third time I achieved a lopsided, brief, feet-in-the-air handstand to the delight of my girls.

Yes, I'm nuts, but we stored up some great family memories that will be treasured my entire life. Vacations were the fun times…but they also were important moments of learning.

Our vacations were never perfect. (Go ahead and admit it: are yours?) There were always downsides to these trips that inevitably held lots of attractions, souvenir shops, and treats. As every parent knows, one of the most stressful days during these family breaks are the "Mommy (or Daddy), can I buy (fill in the blank), can I do (fill in the blank), can I get (fill in the blank)?"

What was the blank? Whatever it was, it cost money. Souvenirs, activities, arcade machines, ice cream—you name it—they wanted to do it all and spend it all. Vacations were like the Niagara Falls of spending.

So Dan and I came up with a plan: Why not give our daughters a budget? We thought we were brilliant. Begin the week with a specific dollar amount that we'd give them in cash, and they would have to be responsible for their own spending. Well, that year Loren was twelve and Chelsea eight, so of course, as parents, whatever rules you create you have to fulfill. Sticking to the rules became the hard part.

My husband and I came up with a plan:
Why not give our daughters a budget?
We thought we were brilliant.

That particular vacation where we came up with the budget philosophy was at a beach resort that had this fun arcade on the grounds, and we allowed our daughters to visit it by themselves. They had the cash in hand that we had given them at the beginning of the week with the rules on what it was meant to be used for. The cash could be completely spent at their discretion, but they were not to ask us for any more money when this ran out.

Inside the arcade was one of those machines with a crane in it that picked up small stuffed animals. If you put in 50 cents and completed the task, grabbing the animal in the claw to successfully drop it into the depository, it was yours. My youngest was enthralled. This machine actually awarded stuffed animals! In the first three days of a weeklong vacation she came home with handfuls of little creatures. What we didn't realize was that, by midweek, she'd spent every cent on this challenge.

Wednesday of our vacation week our family went off the resort location to the local souvenir shops. Store to store we walked, perusing the wares that none of us needed but shopped for nonetheless. After all, it was vacation.

Halfway through our day Chelsea came up to us with a toy she wanted badly.

Our response? "If you have the money, get it."

The "It's up to you" line was received by a stricken look and immediate tears. Chelsea had no money left; she was broke.

Dan and I took her, tears streaming down her face, out of the store to a nearby bench. The sight of my daughter in emotional pain killed me. We found out the child had spent every bit of her money on the arcade and had nothing left for the rest of the week.

As a mom, oh, how I wanted to buy the toy for her, front her some money from her allowance, get her a bank loan, whatever it took. I didn't care. My daughter's heart was breaking.

How I wanted to buy the toy for her,
front her some money from her allowance,
get her a bank loan, whatever it took....

I mean, I somehow managed, at forty, a headstand in the middle of the pool. Surely I could find a way to fix this.

One look at my husband and I silently mouthed *I can't do this.* Then I immediately ran for cover, leaving the two of them to discuss her plight. At that moment I was weak. I knew our daughter needed to learn this lesson, but I was incapable of doing this job. Fortunately, my husband understood my momentary inadequacy and took charge. He explained to her the consequences of her financial decisions and the need to budget her money, as we'd talked about when we'd given it to her. Because she'd already spent her money, she wouldn't be able to buy anything else the rest of the week.

Chelsea cried for a good long while. Finally I got my resolve back, stepped back into the parenting role, comforted her, and we loaded the car to go back to the resort.

I'm glad we stuck to our original plan. But it was only because, at that moment, my husband was better at this job than I was.

What was amazing is the final result. The next trip our family took Chelsea divided her money equally, using six envelopes for each day of the week. She didn't open them until the appropriate day and even managed to come home with money left over. Chelsea had learned firsthand a lesson in budgeting, and it wasn't one she would forget.

Did this one lesson take care of the spending issue in her life? No, it was only one lesson...but it was effective. And it all happened at a time when my desire was just to have a great time with my family, instead of difficult battles and heartbreak. You see, such lessons happen best when we're "in the trenches" of life.

If your school doesn't teach consumer math, do it yourself. Even if they do teach it, review and reinforce this education with your own knowledge. Take the time to instruct your daughters how to buy insurance and why, what a car loan or mortgage is and how much they end up paying in interest, how you use a credit card and what it should be used for. Make a budget.

And do all of this in a way that works for your daughter. Since girls come with different brain cells and talents, you have to personalize this education. When working on budgets with my daughters, one daughter views life details one way and the other girl has an entirely different perspective. So we made the budget accordingly. One understood that things like school supplies, clothing, cosmetics, and cleaning supplies were different categories. The other daughter had a budget line entitled *Target*. She knew how much she could spend at that store, and that's what she did. Both girls learned that using their cash was a lot better than a credit card. When they ran out of money, they knew they had to quit spending. The few times they ran out of funds early was also a great teacher.

When both our daughters went to college, we helped with spending money in the form of a credit card. We were in a position to do this, and we wanted their education to be their primary focus. I learned the hard way how to manage this commitment. Dinner out with all her new friends on Mom's credit card the first month at college brought the wrath of Mom into my elder daughter's life quickly. She was making new friends, she figured, so why shouldn't she buy their meals as well?

I learned the hard way how to manage this commitment.

So I explained again that credit cards were only for agreed to expenditures, not for random use in college life. The only other charges that were to be made were in the event of an emergency, and dinner out with friends was *not* an emergency.

The new policy we decided on was to transfer money into her personal checking account twice a month. She had to pay all personal expenses from this account. She also had to subsidize what we gave her with money she earned to meet this cost.

As our daughters grew older, we transferred more of their overhead to them. Sometimes we helped by increasing our contribution because their earning power was so small. But even though we were still paying for items like health insurance, we did that by adding the money into their income stream from Mom and Dad. Then they had to pay those bills and felt ownership and responsibility by doing so.

Successful Financial Consulting—no matter your financial position—comes down to a few important requirements.

- Begin early.
- Teach financial responsibility by example first, education next.
- Make sure they know that everything offered is not everything needed. You cannot and must not spend more than you have...at least not without consequences.
- Money is not and should never be the great divider. It will only dictate what you can become if you let debt overtake or wealth dominate.
- And finally, money is only a tool, not an answer.

It is your job, Financial Consultant, to teach your daughters to use that tool well. If they do, they'll avoid the end caps, control their credit cards, and learn to manage money well. Money won't manage them.

10

WANTED

Bodyguard

| Job Description |

Usually armed. Responsible for the ongoing safety of one or more persons. Must be able to work as part of a team, as well as independently when required. Must possess great observation skills, the abilities to maintain client confidentiality, to remain calm under pressure, and to defend and protect when safety is threatened. Good planning skills and highly effective interpersonal skills are a must.

I t is 3:00 a.m. in Florida, and our telephone rings. I stumble out of bed and, completely incoherent, pick up the telephone. (I already warned you what I'm like first thing in the morning before I've had two cups of coffee; the middle of the night is worse.) I mumble a hello.

There's a hysterical voice at the other end of the line. Waking up quickly, I realize this is my nineteen-year-old daughter, who is attending college in California. And she's sobbing uncontrollably.

Barely making out her words, I find myself terrified, shouting across 3,000 miles of telephone line to get her to calm down. She gathers herself enough to tell me she has just been in a car accident. Now she's walking beside her car barefoot in broken glass, completely in shock after a front-end collision with another automobile.

My lioness Mom qualities kick in with a vengeance.
Immediately I ask her to sit down. I ask if anyone is with her.
Yes, she has a friend in the car.

Is her friend conscious and seated? Yes, she is.

Has anyone called the police? She doesn't know. I'm the first call she made.

My lioness Mom qualities kick in with a vengeance.

Is anyone else there? A weak, shaky voice tells me that a couple drove up, and they are calling the police now.

What about the driver of the other car? She doesn't know.

Are you bleeding anywhere? Only her feet.

How is your car? "The front end is in the dashboard, Mommy," she says.

My heart drops even further. I stay on the phone with her, trying to remain calm myself to keep her hysteria in check. My husband is sitting up in bed, asking questions that I really don't have the answers to. We are both wishing this moment was a nightmare from which we would awaken.

The police arrive, then the paramedics. I reluctantly get off the telephone, leaving the work to the professionals who have taken charge of the accident site.

I couldn't have felt more helpless. My daughter was just in a major auto accident, and I was 3,000 miles away. You have to understand that my husband and I are not faint-of-heart individuals. We've conquered many obstacles in life, often very difficult ones. But we spent the rest of that night roaming the house between telephone calls feeling completely helpless, knowing we had not one ounce of control over this moment in our daughter's life. There was nothing we could do, and we were in agony.

I have never felt as lost as I did that night. You see, it was my job to protect her. I am her mother.

When a daughter is born, there are two instantaneous emotions: one is love; the other is protection. For me, both were immediate and equally fierce. I was capable of any defense, should someone ever attempt to hurt my girls. I knew at their birth that there was nothing I would not stand against to protect these precious babies. They were mine to keep from harm.

So in the real world of daughter duties, are we equipped to be the person who would take the bullet? The valiant, without-a-second-thought bodyguard who leaps in front of the danger heading straight for the heart of our daughters?

The simple answer is yes, we are.

There was nothing I would not stand against to protect these precious babies.

Do we leap into the line of fire? Yes, we do.

Are we always supposed to take that bullet? Stop right there. Now the answer is no.

Do we tackle the offender? Sometimes yes, and sometimes no.

Are we to allow our charges to take a few knocks themselves? Yes, indeed we are.

Are you confused yet? In this job there are multiple correct answers. You see, the answers change based upon the timeline in your daughter's life, the danger present, and each individual objective.

Here's what I mean. Sometimes the bullets come when your toddler is deadheading toward an open flame and you throw yourself in front of your child, extinguishing the threat. Or you see a car driving down your street as your four-year-old is running after her ball and you perform a body lunge toward her, pulling her from harm. If the danger comes in the form of a boy or a friend, you may have to let your girl take some pain. When she enters the years behind the wheel, you can only be there through the student-driver stage. Then she leaves home for college, and suddenly you can no longer protect her.

If you want to do this job well, you have three goals. First, it is your job to protect. Second, you are to teach them to protect themselves. And finally, if successful, you will have prepared her to protect those she loves as well. The end of a job well done is that your duty will be over. You will be able to retire and relax. After all, when you get arthritic knees, you certainly don't want to try to outrun a grown daughter just to protect her.

Assessing the Dangers

What does this bodyguard job look like, and what do you have to do? It's easy to envision the human mannequins you've seen in multiple movies, as well as all political events with presidents or presidential candidates. You know, the menacing guys wearing sunglasses, suit, and tie, with an earpiece in their ear and a gun in a holster. They're standing completely still while discretely scanning for any and all potential dangers.

These are intimidating agents who have learned how to be effective at their job. They shoot well, granted. They are physically fit to run toward danger. They look really impressive in their suits. (I don't think that makes a lot of difference, but I couldn't resist the observation.) Their powers of surveillance must be vulture-like. Those great sunglasses are proof of that! All of these, except maybe the suits, apply.

But the most important ability for the mom version of this bodyguard is the talent of observation. Keep an eye out for any and all potential harm. Assess its intent and determine the best course of action. Then take the next step to protect or prepare.

The threat that is most spoken of for girls today, the one that brings heartbreak to every mother, is the danger from sexual predators. We see it played out in the media, and it grips all of our hearts with anger and fear. We have learned that this menace comes from people familiar to us, as well those we simply don't know. An effective bodyguard isn't fooled that this predator is always an elusive stranger.

When my girls were small, I found this job a difficult balance. While I wanted to educate my daughters to be wary of predators, I also wanted to teach them kindness to all. I didn't want them to replace compassion, vulnerability, and the ability to reach out to others with fear.

If an individual approaches your daughter, saying he lost his puppy, what heartstrings are pulled? Is this a real need of a stranger—or a person with ulterior motives? You want compassion to be your daughter's natural instinct while teaching her to recognize the circumstances.

Does the stranger's request make sense—or not? If the request comes from a child, then the dog may truly be lost, and the child may truly need help. But if an adult is asking for help, teach your daughter to find another adult. She needs to understand that adults assist other adults; children don't. Place logic into her mind instead of fear. Offer the wisdom of caution and the simple steps she needs to take to ensure she will be safe.

Effective Weapons

The most effective weapon in your daughter's arsenal is confidence. This is not just a theory from a mother. A study of criminal behavior in the *Psychology Today* article "Marked for Mayhem" revealed possible deterrents to physical attack. Repeatedly they were told by the criminals interviewed that they were looking for and preying upon those who appear weak, vulnerable, and easily controlled. These became their most likely target. It has been proven time and again that self-confidence works. If your daughter holds her head high, eyes straight ahead, she will look less vulnerable to a predator. If approached, she will act decisively. Without meekness, the chances of an attack drop precipitously. Predators traditionally are not strong humans; they are looking to create strength over the weaker. If your daughter possesses self-confidence, she is armed.

If your daughter possesses self-confidence, she is armed.

Help her understand she must always "trust her gut." If she feels something is wrong, if it seems odd or out of place, back away. A child's instinct is reliable. Her best plan is to listen to the first warning bell and act. She will never look back in dismay on the times she thought something was wrong and acted upon her instinct even while feeling foolish in her reaction. She'll only regret the times she doesn't listen to her instincts in facing danger.

Taking a bullet is easier for you when your daughter is little. You see the stove, hear the car coming, and know the pool is too deep. When your daughter gets older, taking the bullet can become more difficult. The teen years bring a time of protection in a different form. Your powers of observation have to be even more astute, your line of defense more varied.

Somewhere between twelve and seventeen years of age almost all girls will find a boy or make a friend who potentially brings with him or her a whole bunch of problems.

I hit this milestone with Loren when she was thirteen. She had a friend she met in middle school, and that friend didn't live by any rules. The girl was fun, I liked her, but my insight told me this girl was headed for trouble. The girl's mother had a pretty loose reign on her. The thirteen-year-old was left alone in her home until 2 a.m., allowed to date at that age—and allowed to date boys much older than she was.

The girl had very few responsibilities or expectations placed on her in any part of her life. This freedom, along with the fact the girl was really cute and fun, held an irresistible allure for Loren.

Feeling this wasn't the best relationship for my daughter, I tried to impede their friendship. But with each attempt I made to curtail this connection, the deeper it became. I was in a losing battle...until I changed my tactical maneuvers. I began to embrace this girl's presence in our lives. I invited her everywhere on behalf of my daughter: to spend the night, for shopping expeditions, on our day trips, to church, or anyplace else I could make it fit.

Let me be clear: I'm not saying this girl was "the enemy"; she was only a child. But the life she was allowed to live posed a danger to my daughter's well-being. So I took the tact of "keeping my enemies closer."

It didn't take much time before my daughter started making irritated comments about this newfound friendship. Way too much exposure tarnished the sheen. When her friend was in our world, away from the "glamour" of hers, she didn't seem quite as nice and exciting. Soon their friendship began to fizzle.

I took the tact of "keeping my enemies closer."

When I asked Loren if her friend would be joining us, the answer began to be no. The excitement and appeal had faded. The threat had been removed without a throw-down pronouncement by Mom. Had I continued on the road of confrontation, I would have lost. But I protected my daughter in another way.

I cannot guarantee there won't be times when you just have to hit the mat to win the battle. There will be. But if you can find another route toward success, it's less painful for all.

Nothing in Life Is Fail-Proof

Protecting your daughter from her own bad decisions isn't fail-proof. Your girl is indeed an individual with her own free will. We teach our children how to treat burns if they happen, how to call the police and exchange information if in an auto accident. We try to instill the value of the 9-1-1 telephone call, which of course my nineteen-year-old didn't use. In her panic, she did the only thing she could remember to do: she called home. We do well when we provide very practical instruction for the simple problems.

Protection from your daughter's life bad decisions requires much more. Sometimes tactical maneuvers work; sometimes they don't. Our daughters will make bad decisions; we are foolish if we think they won't. I certainly made my own in life, and you can't tell me in all honesty that you missed out on that one yourself.

So here's your goal: do your best to help your daughter not make a decision that changes the course of her life. Becoming pregnant, contracting an STI, having an auto accident with personal injury or death, drinking or drugs that alter the consequences of one night—these and more are the places you hope to never find your daughter.

That's why discipline and rules are mandatory. I call this *passive protection*. The best way to assist your daughter in making a minimum of bad decisions is to limit her exposure. Help her avoid scenarios that introduce her to compromise.

When I was seventeen, my weekend curfew was midnight. I had friends who were allowed to stay out past that hour, so I fought my parents valiantly and nonstop to change that rule. They would not bend. One night, when arguing again with my father, he posed a question to me: "What can you do or where can you go after 12:00 that doesn't lead to trouble?"

I stumbled. Movies were over, concerts had let out, ball games and school dances were done. I could say, "Just hang out with my friends," but I knew that wouldn't fly. I couldn't give him a good answer because there wasn't one.

My curfew remained, and that day I quit arguing. My father was smart; he kept me from making bad decisions by limiting the opportunity.

*One night, when arguing again with
my father, he posed a question to me:
"What can you do or where can you go
after 12:00 that doesn't lead to trouble?"*

The questions my own teenage daughters always had to answer were: Where are you going, with whom, and what time will it be over? They had to provide the detail before they left home, and if plans changed, they had telephones and were instructed to inform us immediately. Information was king at the Brock Family Home.

I also told them I knew they could tell me in great detail what their plans were and the moment they left the house they could be anywhere with anyone doing anything. Without a satellite-tracking device or an accidental meeting, I wouldn't know the difference. So I told our daughters that Part One of our policy was that they were implicitly given our trust—that we believed they would always tell us the truth.

But there was a Part Two to that policy: should we ever find out they lied to us, that trust would be lost...and it would be a long, agonizing journey to ever regain it.

The choice was theirs.

Setting reasonable, easily understood, and concrete rules for curfews, age-appropriate entertainment, what friends can be in the car, seatbelt use, and other oversight is important in your parental role.

But as you set the rules, also be willing to listen. Be reasonable and rational. If her curfew is midnight, and she has worked at the fast-food restaurant until close at 9 p.m., allow her to make a presentation. She and her friends are getting a burger, then going to the 10:20 movie premiere that they have all been waiting to see. With drive time, which means not speeding and dropping off her best friend, she can't make it home until 12:45.

Should you stick with the rules because they are the rules? Say, "No, absolutely not. 12:45 is past your curfew!"? Your daughter has a job, for heaven's sake! She is being responsible and presenting her case. So give it to her! Your focus should be on building mutual respect and training her to become an adult, not merely setting rules that must be rigidly adhered to.

The day will arrive when she will be on her own; she must be prepared to provide her own protection. Helping her build good decision-making skills will help her do this. Part of bending your rules when appropriate creates the ability in your daughter to make these good decisions.

Preparation Is Your Best Defense

If you have ever watched dog trainers, they keep the dog on a short leash until they learn. Then slowly, over time, the dogs are given room to maneuver.

The same is true with our daughters: you want to give them the ability to make their own decisions. The rules made at thirteen aren't the same as at age fifteen, which aren't the same as at age eighteen. I've seen many kids who were raised in the most stable homes hit college and party until the sun comes up. Why? Because they were overprotected and underexposed. They weren't allowed to experience life, pain, and just grow up. They weren't prepared for the sudden freedom thrust upon them. Instead of experiencing decision making while they were in their parents' home, they only experienced being told what to do, and when. Now suddenly they were free to do whatever they wanted without anyone at home seeing what was going on.

There are times when protection against life's hurt, consequence, and injustice is a job we moms shouldn't perform (as much as it kills us to watch our daughters suffer). We are just as irresponsible when we overprotect our daughters as when we choose to underprotect them. It is normal for a mother to want no hurt in the life of her children. We hurt when they hurt. But preventing any heartache or difficulty in your daughter's life stunts her ability to live in a difficult world. A bodyguard protects, but if she is really good, she also teaches self-defense.

We mothers often fear rejection from our daughters too much. When they are clamoring to get out on their own, we take it personally. A bodyguard? He or she just moves on to a new job. Hard to do that as a mother, isn't it? But there's something to be learned about this role. While we really will miss our daughters when they leave, we *want* them to leave. And no, I don't mean getting them out of the house so they're no longer underfoot (though some days, in the heat of the moment, that might be a bonus). Instead, we want them to be complete, competent humans who can make it on their own.

> *A bodyguard protects, but if she is really good,*
> *she also teaches self-defense.*

But to get them ready takes years of preparation. Your daughter can't wake up one day and leave home ready to meet the world. You have to teach her life skills. Not a one of us wants our daughters to suffer heartache, disappointment, and punishment, but here's the catch: they *must.* We cannot forever insulate our daughters from the sadness and evil of our world. They have to experience childhood peer rejection, pain, and distress to prepare them for adult peer rejection, pain, and distress.

Allowing them in the right season to gain insight on other people, as well as knowledge of society, is necessary preparation for independence. We cannot come between them and life, because most of life lessons are learned through experience. Those lessons cannot be explained or instructed, they have to be lived. As much as we would like, our daughters cannot be raised in a bubble, then thrust into the real world and expected to handle it. We have to train them much as you do an athlete. Each time they gain ability, they are taught a new skill. The old "no pain no gain" applies to emotional strength as much as physical strength.

I have a limited view of running. It would only become necessary in my life should I be chased. Fear of harm is the only thing that would drive me to run. I can't think of another good reason to get my legs going that fast. It simply doesn't make one iota of sense to me. Yet I love watching runners at the Olympic Games. They are so lean, muscular, disciplined, and determined. When they run, it looks so effortless. They *fly*.

The ultimate fun is the 4 x 100 relay. This is a combination of four runners, each set appropriately in position to make the most of their running ability to then hand off the baton to the subsequent runner for their leg. The race ends with everyone rooting for the final competitor sprinting for the finish line. But to win, it takes all team participants excelling at their leg of the race and completing the hand-off to the next runner flawlessly. They have to train and train well to be a part of this team.

Initially, it requires them to become one of the best runners individually. Strength and speed are achieved as they go through levels of training. Beginning naturally at a slower speed, they practice running and achieve endurance. Then they undergo weight training to gain strength to ensure that the body's muscles are powerful enough to maintain the demands placed upon them. After becoming a proficient runner competing individually, they vie for the privilege of being a member of the relay.

The runners look to instruction to determine what place in the race they are most suited for. Training again but no longer alone, they work to perfect the handoff of the baton. This process takes time, commitment, and determination by the runner and coaching by an effective instructor. Finally after years of preparation they become a cohesive team that can function smoothly as one entity.

In the same way, you as mom go from the pure taking of the bullet to teaching self-defense. Then you move from teaching defense to committed character building. You, Mom, are one leg of the race, and your goal is to train your daughter to be strong enough to run her leg of the race well.

One of the final stages of bodyguard protection and preparation comes in the nuances of society—the areas of life that can be difficult to define and where gray areas often seem appropriate.

Train your daughter to be strong enough to run her leg of the race well.

We Brocks were parents who demanded and expected personal responsibility from ourselves as well as our children. So when faced with our younger daughter's interest in taking an Ethics Class at the local college, we had apprehensions.

Chelsea was a senior in high school, completing her education at an "institution of higher learning"—the college in our community. We were savvy enough to know that the ethics being taught at the public institution would in no way resemble our position or values, but she wanted to take the class so, with some trepidation, we signed on.

The course description included absolute and relative systems, ethical issues in contemporary society, defining ethical judgments and refining them. We could have run from this influence, but we determined it would challenge her and prepare her for many life confrontations in the area of ethical or moral stances.

Before she began, we discussed the possibilities of the course work and what would be taught. She listened (I'm sure mentally rolling her eyes, thinking we were so overreacting). Then began the class. Indeed she was taught that there are no moral absolutes because what is considered correct in one culture is not in another, so how could any one set of rules be right? The issues of life value and religious influence on moral culture and its relevance were addressed, as well as questions such as, "Is a lie ever appropriate?"

We had many discussions at our home regarding these subjects. When is it right to take another person's life? I had to admit that if anyone was trying to take my child from my home to inflict harm that would be the time I'd be tempted to take a life.

Is it ever okay to lie? Those who saved lives during the Holocaust lied, yet their cause was nobler than truth. They saved others from torture and death by their deceit.

In hindsight, I'm delighted Chelsea took the class. It challenged her. She worked through many issues. Not all were completely resolved, but they were weighed. It would have been wrong to run from something we thought was dangerous to our daughter's moral character. You see, Chelsea has always been a child who makes discoveries, seeks information, and constantly wants to learn. She is curious about other people's opinions—how they formed them and why. This subject was no different. It was not a denouncement of all she had been taught from us, but a step toward creating and confirming her own thoughts as she grew toward adulthood.

If our daughter didn't face the issues in that class, at a time when she could discuss her thoughts and questions with us, in the safe setting of our home, we knew that she would address them later, in another time, in another way. And later she might not have the support of others who shared our family's values. So we were there as parents in an open forum, discussing all she was learning. We did resolve many of the questions she developed during this course study because we allowed that opportunity in her life while were by her side.

Through the exercises and discussions, we didn't always agree. Chelsea had her own opinions. What's even crazier is that she was right in some of those disagreements. Remember: you want a daughter, not a clone. She must figure out the issues for herself, but if you do your job, her judgments will be more often right than wrong.

Your Job Is to Protect—At All Costs

Overprotection is a problem, but complete destruction comes from others who have discarded the responsibility to protect. News stories tell of many mothers who allow physical abuse in their home. They may choose a husband, boyfriend, or relative over their daughters, feeling helpless to change a dangerous situation. Looking the other way, they abandon their first priority: to protect their daughters. It is in no one's best interest to remain in a place where violence, physical or verbal, is dispensed. This is destructive not only to the mother but to the entire family and must end.

I watch as the entertainment industries seek increasingly younger performers. I am astounded by the mothers who encourage their daughters in the fields of performance, often allowing their girls to set aside self-esteem for "success." Placing a vulnerable child in the way of a manipulative entertainment industry without guarding their best interest is unforgivable.

Child stars are often damaged by the world they are exposed to when their parents quit being parents. I'm not saying you should deny your child the opportunity that may be right for who she is to become. But it's imperative you remain the *parent* in that world. Children are still-developing humans who require protect-tion, rules, discipline, education, and simple fun to grow up to be functioning adults. Industry standards should never supersede parental standards in a child's life, no matter how "successful" she is. The first rule of order is that the parent rules—no one else.

Children are sometimes left completely alone to care for themselves. The damage done when a child is unattended while a mother goes elsewhere, seeking her own pleasure and fulfillment, is unconscionable. I want to be clear that this is not a commentary on the *working* mother (after all, I was one myself all the years my daughters were growing up) but on the *selfish* mother, who is acting solely for her own best interests and not considering what is best for her child.

The first rule of order is that the parent rules—
no one else.

I find myself equally incensed by the mothers who exploit their daughters, using them to gain income. I am not speaking of pure prostitution but encouraging seductively inappropriate behavior for cash. Some moms have gone as far as allowing their girls to film themselves provocatively at thirteen years of age to be displayed on the internet. One of these mothers justified her actions by saying, "We are saving this money so my daughter can go to college one day."

Money, college, or any other "perk" will mean nothing to our daughters' futures if we allow their self-worth to be torn down by our lack of commonsense and protection.

The Secret Service of the United States of America has a valiant statement of core values, reflecting an oath and commitment we can use for the position of Mother Bodyguard:

Each point of the Secret Service star represents one of the agency's five core values: justice, duty, courage, honesty and loyalty. These values, and the Secret Service motto "Worthy of Trust and Confidence," resonate with each man and woman who has sworn the oath to uphold them. To reinforce these values, Secret Service leaders and employees promote and measure personal accountability and program performance across the agency. By holding each person to the highest standards of personal and professional integrity, the Secret Service ensures the preservation of its core values, the fulfillment of its vision and the success of its mission.[3]

[3] http://www.secretservice.gov/FY2008_AnnualReport_WM.pdf.

It is the same with a mother and daughter. When we choose to accept the job of Bodyguard, protecting and conducting ourselves in the best interest of our children, we will be successful. Note that I said *success*. Not perfection. Not without failure or setbacks. But success in the long-term with rearing a daughter who will be a healthy and balanced person who contributes to our world in positive ways.

Bodyguards in other professions have to sign an oath. So why shouldn't mothers have to sign an oath when birthing or adopting a child? We moms must intentionally choose to conduct ourselves "worthy of trust and confidence."

We moms must intentionally choose
to conduct ourselves
"worthy of trust and confidence."

So, Bodyguard, how do we protect and prepare?

Do we leap into the line of fire? Yes, we do.

Are we always supposed to take that bullet? No.

Do we always tackle the offender? Yes and no.

Do we allow our charge to take a few knocks herself? Yes.

You must protect, teach, and prepare your daughter, then send her off to fulfill her destiny with the ability to manage life well without you by her side. And here's the long-term perk for you: if you do that, you are out of a job—at least one of them, Bodyguard.

11

WANTED
Communications Specialist

| Job Description |

Mastery in the art of communication: responsible for the application of techniques used to apply words effectively. Able to provide instruction in the tools needed to successfully impart information or ideas. Must possess the ability to transmit information to ensure open, interactive, and effective communication skills.

We, the female gender, have been given a special talent. We are amazing at the ability to communicate, to impart information, to secure effect. We use words in abundance. If we are honest, what we really use is paragraphs, not sentences, or we complete sentences, not just words.

We can convince others of our point of view or encourage someone to action with the sheer quantity of information that comes out of our mouths. Sometimes I believe it may not be the amazing content but the pure volume itself. Surrender may come out of nothing less than exhaustion on the part of those we are speaking to.

You see, words are our strength. They are also our weakness. If not used correctly, this gift can be the most damaging human weapon known to humankind. Since our verbal ability is instinctive, we often use words without thought, leaving a path of destruction we may not even see. We might pride ourselves in the ability to say what is on our mind, without holding back. We might believe that it is our responsibility to set things straight...no matter what. Yet when words are wielded effectively as a sword over someone else, they can leave in their wake devastation, humiliation, hurt, and heartbreak.

Words are our strength.
They are also our weakness.

Words are very much a lethal weapon, and all women know their strength. That's why it's critical we become Communications Specialists early, training ourselves in the art of speaking. Otherwise our own words can cause death. I'm not speaking of the end of our physical existence, but the death of relationships, opportunity, friendship, and family strength. All in life that is good and valuable can be degraded by thoughtless remarks or by purposeful comments that have veiled but malicious intent.

The Wisdom of Solomon

King Solomon, whom I continue to be fascinated by, appeared to have absolutely no understanding of women. Marrying as many women as he did and keeping them all around in a harem solidifies the fact that the wisest man who ever lived was at least at some point in life clueless.

Can you imagine the things said among Solomon's wives at the harem?

"Oh, that haircut looks wonderful. It's a very appropriate style for a woman of *your* age."

Or maybe something like this: "That was such a thoughtless remark from her. Oh, you didn't hear it? Well, just know *I* would never have said that about you."

Then imagine the harem concern for another in their ranks: "We're so dismayed about how she raises that son. The way she pampers him"—heads shake—"and to think he is supposed to be the king's heir. It's so sad that he certainly won't be fit for the throne."

Can you imagine the things said among Solomon's wives at the harem?

And the one wife to another wife (if our brain can even go there) statement: "I overheard the eunuch, and he said I'm the king's favorite. I don't know why he likes me so much when you're so special too."

A conclave of women vying for importance in the royal household would have been filled with conniving, dangerous, and unbelievably ugly words cloaked in prettiness. Yet the sole husband of all those wives expounded some of the most amazing wisdom, proving that somewhere in life he came to understand these creatures he brought into his kingdom. His observations regarding women and the effect of their words are profound.

Take these for example:

A quarrelsome wife is like a dripping faucet.
In other words: Constant nagging is seriously irritating, and anyone living with that would pay a plumber any amount of money to make it stop.

Better to live on the corner of the roof than share a house with a quarrelsome woman.
In other words: Your husband, sitting in his easy chair in front of the big screen TV, is contemplating that living on the roof in the rain would be better than hearing you complain about one more thing.

Better to live in the desert than with a contentious and angry wife.

In other words: A dry, sandy, hot, miserable desert lined with cacti looks like a great place to be when arguing and dissatisfaction is the only thing that ever comes out of your wife's mouth.

The Misuse of Words

We are delighted when our baby girls add to their vocabulary in their own special way. They form words that only we can decipher. The sentences they create begin with one word, then two or three words, then move to whole sentences, and finally, never-ending paragraphs. It's when the words get strung together that things can get ugly. The sweet "mommy, doggie, teddy bear" words turn into "no, I don't want to; get me down; that's mine"—all said, of course, at the top of their lungs.

Effective Communications Specialists realize that defiant, resistant phrases have to be addressed at that very early age. It's not only the words our daughters learn but what lies behind them.

When you are unloading the car and she is impatient to get out of the car seat, she must ask, not scream and demand. A child who barks commands to her mother and gets by with it is being trained to be controlling. The art of effective communication is learning *how* to say things to accomplish the results you want.

If we respond to demands acting upon our daughters' directive, they will learn this is the way to get whatever they want. Then the only forms of request your child knows are screaming, demanding, and insisting, and I can guarantee you she will use those to the very best of her ability.

So teach your child not only *how* to ask—nicely—for what she wants but also make it clear there is a time she needs to stop asking, even if the answer you give isn't what she wants to hear. It may look like, to others, that you are merely trying to curb the attitude of a little one, but it is much more than that. An adult woman will communicate using whichever communication skills she's been taught and developed throughout her growing-up years. It's one thing for a two-year-old to demand action loudly and belligerently; it's a whole other thing for a forty-two-year-old to do it.

It just ain't pretty.

No!

This simple two-letter English word can be the most rebellious statement made by your precious two-year-old. Granted, that word has been a constant one she's heard for the last eighteen months from you, the mother. The first time she reaches for something harmful, you say no. When she pulls your hair, you say no. When she throws food across the kitchen, you say no.

But your daughter's no is done with a different kind of attitude. When she looks straight into your eyes after you ask her to pick up her toys and says, "No!" you feel the full impact of her defiance. What does her "No!" really mean? It means, "Ain't no way, Mama, and I absolutely dare you to make me do it."

What does her "No!" really mean?
It means, "Ain't no way, Mama, and I
absolutely dare you to make me do it."

What does verbal defiance, if not curbed in childhood, accomplish for an adult woman? It gets her nowhere. Others avoid her, pacify her, and skirt around her issues rather than engaging. So now's the time to nip "No" in the bud, no matter what age your daughter is.

Mine!

Mine is a simple, four-letter, possessive pronoun. But it speaks volumes. One of my daughters had a cloth doll that went everywhere with her. During the day it was dragged around the house; it was always in her bed at night. My daughter and that doll were inseparable. She would lay in bed twirling her hair, saying, "Lolly doll is my friend. She is my baby" and other sweet, endearing phrases.

It was in day care that I first saw the other version of "mine" from little this girl. As I walked into the class to pick her up, a little boy reached for her doll.

And from my sweet angel's lips came an ear-piercing shriek: "MIIIINNNNE!!!" (Note triple exclamation marks.) Quickly picking up the toy truck he had left behind, she promptly hit him over the head to make sure he understood the meaning of that word.

From my sweet angel's lips came an ear-piercing shriek: "MIIIINNNNE!!!"

He did. Then he cried as I strode across the playroom, scooped my daughter up, and scolded her action. I tried to make my daughter understand that this behavior was completely unacceptable and made it clear that she needed to tell him she was sorry and ask for forgiveness from the little boy.

After that process, the little boy settled down and appeared relatively unscathed, so my daughter and I went home to continue this discussion, as well as pursue the appropriate discipline for her action. The intention behind this word then was anything but endearment. It was selfish vehemence on my girl's part.

The "mine" in an adult female is present in both hearts and vocabularies. But it's most often couched in sentences so innocuous that they are often unidentifiable. It's not the obvious screeching of a demanding little girl across the playroom but said about something we want that is only in our desire or best interest.

I believe in my husband's and my wedding vows we should have added "I, Darlene, will never add floral prints, lace curtains, or girlie colors in our home." Now I'm not a floral-print, lacey kind of female, but if I was, my husband would have been miserable in his own home. I've seen that kind of décor in homes where a hunting, fishing, spitting kind of guy resides. I really believe that screams "mine" in the grown-up world, because truly the home front should be the epitome of marital compromise and unselfish actions. It doesn't matter how many times you say or convince yourself the home is beautiful, if it is beautiful only to you.

"I want what I want and nothing less" can be delivered with a smile, by stubbornness, through sex, through stony silence, or other ways a female can use to make clear what she wants and to get her way.

So when you find yourself falling into such behavior, take a step back. Is the possessive, selfish intention of your presentation clear? Do you want this just because your intent is "mine"—or because it's the right thing to do for your family?

The "no" and "mine" are all simple word lessons to be taught when your child is young and just beginning the verbal barrages. As in every other life instruction you give to your daughter, managing the words she uses must come early, consistently reinforcing how you want her to speak.

Belittling

I believe that all women every day of their lives have to battle the misuse of words. Words are something we are so good at that we will always fall prey to abuse. The biggest teacher to our daughters will be the very words we speak.

Back to the words of Solomon: *A wise woman builds her house, but with her own hands a foolish one tears hers down.*

In other words: Often our homes are destroyed by us. Never

do we bring in the bulldozer, raise the sledgehammer, or wield the ax; it is our words that we use to accomplish the demolition. It is those words our daughters must be instructed to guard against.

There are many things said by mothers that make me sad. One of the most distressful is hearing a mother belittling her child. The casual or angry phrases we are capable of speaking destroy our daughters' self-confidence and decry the relationship of love between a child and their mother.

I'm not saying we should tell them constantly they are beautiful, brilliant, and perfect 24/7. They aren't. But we should not demean their look, their actions, or their words. We should build them up. We can help our daughters rise above difficult circumstances simply by our support and love. What they think of themselves will greatly be based upon what we have said to them.

If we say they are smart, they will believe they are.

If we say they are stupid, they will believe that as well.

If we tell them they can accomplish a difficult task, they will believe they can.

If we tell them a challenge is too much for them, they will believe that, too.

What they think of themselves will greatly be based upon what we have said to them.

Many women speak to their husbands or about their husbands with superiority and disdain. Words that disparage the character and nature of a man only serve to destroy the promising relationship that began on their day of commitment. As much as it is true that a man needs his wife to believe in him, it is equally true that if a wife's words indicate contempt, a husband is left with two choices. The first is to live his life seeking, at all costs, to make peace in his home—subsequently losing himself in the process. The second is to look elsewhere for someone who encourages his self-worth.

Words are powerful—far more powerful than you could ever imagine. And the consequences of your words are far-reaching in every area of life, but especially in the arena of family.

So let me be blunt. Since we, as women, are often motivated by self- preservation, why would we *choose* to drive a husband away by our words? After all, you can absolutely count on the fact that there is a woman in your husband's life who is willing and desiring to fulfill whatever he is seeking. A sure way to destroy a marriage is to change from treating the man you married as the life treasure you were seeking to debris that is without value and easily discarded.

And always remember: how you speak to your daughter's father will most likely be how your daughter speaks to her husband. You by your words will serve to prepare her for success or failure in her relationships. If you are not currently married, don't skim over this section. Your daughter does have a father who is a vital part of her life. Your words to him should be words you don't ever regret. This applies to your relationships with all men. Building good relationships is based upon these same principles, and the effect will be the same.

> *How you speak to your daughter's father will most likely be how your daughter speaks to her husband.*

The gossip line

Finally, there is the friend that betrays another, words that are unkind, or gossip shared with someone else for reasons that can never be justified. Women deliver these words. They are cloaked with concern when the motivation is not that whatsoever. The classic phrase "I'm so concerned about Susan" is frequently followed with information about Susan that should never be shared...successfully cloaking gossip in false compassion. And I hate the next phrase that often follows with people of faith: "I wanted you to know so you could pray for her." Now REALLY, this should drive any kindhearted woman into insanity. We can pray without ever knowing all the details!

All women have been the victim of the "kind words" that really mean something else from other women. These are some of the most hurtful of all, because others who shouldn't know anything about your situation are suddenly informed of the blow-by-blow details, all under the guise of "helping you."

And don't fool yourself: every woman is capable of forming them. That means even you, even me, even your daughter. Used to manipulate a situation or debase another, these are the most effective, while seeming innocuous. They usually begin with Part A, the good side, and end with Part B, the dangerous side.

"That dress makes you look so much thinner than normal." Which is it exactly? Do I look thin or normally look fat?

"I love your new hair color. It's so much better than the old one." So, did you really hate my hair before?

"Your kids behave so well at school." Does that mean they are a mess while you are in your living room or at the mall? Is the teacher better than you with your child? So, what exactly are you saying here?

These examples are a few of the fairly mild sentences that can confuse and unnerve the one being spoken to. Often these are said without thinking or without the perceived intent, but we should guard against these as well. We females of all ages are frequently an insecure bunch, and a thoughtless remark can send an emotionally stable lady into a tailspin. Your daughters instinctively manage these words as you have yourself. Just make sure you teach them that Part A is always good enough on its own.

A thoughtless remark can send
an emotionally stable lady into a tailspin.

The ultimate application of Communications Specialists is this: Do not let your daughter *ever* speak to you using words that you would never say to her. The words used, as well as the attitudes behind those words, must fit this criterion. Adopting this home policy will not only help your daughter think through her words but will make you conscious of yours.

I'm not saying there won't be angry days from both sides of the family. My daughters have stomped up the stairs declaring they are really mad at me.

My response? "Well, no problem whatsoever, because I'm really mad at you too." Anger, frustration, and disagreement are not wrong; it's what is said at those moments that can damage.

Your words bring life or death in the relationship between a mother and daughter.

The Power of Words

I love the statement made by British writer Dorothy Nevill that brings the value of words to life: "The real art of conversation is not only to say the right thing at the right moment but to leave unsaid the wrong thing at the tempting moment."

The reason our words have such impact is because we were made to communicate. We have the amazing ability to change the world. We can persuade as effectively for good. There have been countless women in history who have understood this power and mastered words to achieve a needed end. Let me give you a few amazing examples of how true that can be.

Harriet Beecher Stowe

Harriet Beecher Stowe, author of *Uncle Tom's Cabin,* written in 1852, used her ability to communicate to solidify the residents of the North against slavery. She recognized an injustice, then followed the dictum of her father, who said, "If you see a wrong, right it."

"If you see a wrong, right it."
—HARRIET BEECHER STOWE'S FATHER

It was one Sunday afternoon that Harriett passionately put on paper the story inspired by a vision she received in church that very morning. This work when completed portrayed slaves as human beings that were no less significant and purposed than their white counterparts. Selling 300,000 copies in its first year the publication quickly achieved its goal. Ms. Stowe's work began the course of developing understanding, each race was truly equal helping set the platform that would bring change. Her words on paper activated the north to right this wrong.

Laura Ingalls Wilder

Laura Ingalls Wilder, writer of the *Little House on The Prairie* series along with her daughter/editor, released the first book in 1932. These books portrayed the pioneer culture and the hardships that forged opportunity in our land. In a creative and entertaining way we found ourselves walking through a time lost to our nation. That mental journey mirrored strength of character in a land settled through determination. Today the simplicity of the era portrayed in these books still inspires young generations to dream of life different from what they know and believing they too can forge new paths.

Flannery O'Connor

Author Flannery O'Connor has used the American novel to explore human alienation and the relationship with an individual

God. Depicting the tragic nature of humanity, she profoundly succeeds in challenging the most secure of thinkers. Her work, while sometimes sad and forlorn, creates thought-provoking questions that cry out for answers.

Words of life

Words can bring change, provide comfort, understanding, security, strength, and resolve. These and many other American authors, speakers, and women from all walks of life have changed the country we live in with only their words. Masterfully creating awareness and inspiring reflection, these communicators convince others to believe in themselves. They stir the hearts of many who then become catalysts for change in the world around them.

Words of life are what we want to communicate to our daughters. We must also teach them how to use such words of life—as well as when to speak and when to say nothing. Phrases and sentences should be spoken that encourage others to seek purpose, to feel valued, and to be loved. These will be instructive and corrective when stated in a well-thought-out, humble manner. And not only the ability to speak but the ability to listen will make our words much more valuable. If you have taught this to your daughter, she will be made better by her own words and others will benefit from them as well.

It was the living room of my great grandmother's home on Saturday nights where I waxed most eloquent at five years of age. I'd be standing at the small podium she owned directly in front of the red horsehair sofa. With great flourish and drama I would place the family Bible upon the lectern, opening it to some page (I didn't yet know how to read). There I began my Saturday night sermons.

The stories would grow, taking many turns and forms. I would raise my voice like the preacher I heard in Sunday morning church and expound. My finger would point in the air, my arms would flail. I would walk beside the "pulpit" with confidence to make my point, then return back to the text, staring intently at the page I could not read.

My diminutive grandmother would sit in her housedress with hands in her lap, eyes glued to my every move. She listened attentively. As my stories got bigger and grander, she would nod and agree. When I became quiet and thoughtful in my delivery, she seemed to hang on every word I said. My prose was windy, often confused in direction, but always filled with adjectives. I believed I was the great orator and my audience was enthralled.

And when I was done, I walked away with far more than just knowing I'd made a good presentation that day.

My grandmother treated what I had to say as important, worthy of her time and attention. She made me feel that every word I said mattered. I believed, in those moments, that I had something to share that was worthy of attention...that *I* was worthy of notice. Her attention gave me the confidence that my words could change the world.

She made me feel that every word I said mattered.

The truth is, words can. Communications Specialist, be that lady who sits on the sofa listening. Or let your daughter chatter in the kitchen during meal preparation, expounding on whatever she values that day. If your daughter believes her words matter, and learns how they are to be used for the good, they will have immense impact. Then she, indeed, can change the world. Just watch her!

12

W<small>ANTED</small>
In-home Demonstrator

| Job Description |

Professionally arrange, display, and present products in household venues to illustrate quality of the product line and how it should be used. Effectively communicate the need for and value of the product presented.

"**M**om on Strike!" Through time, mothers have had the urge to strike: to walk out on the job and renegotiate for better terms. Placing a placard in the front lawn of a normal home in Middle America sounds so very appealing sometimes, doesn't it? This large sign could be set to remain front and center until changes are made in your family's life.

Well, that's exactly what the mother of a dear friend of mine did. She placed that sign in her front yard. It remained for more than one month while she went on strike.

Late one night, as we young mothers were weary and expounding on the happenings of our day, my friend told me this tale about her mother. She explained that she didn't understand why her mother did what she did while she was young. But now that she had children of her own, what her mom had done all those years ago finally made sense.

This was the act of a mother desperate for change. A mother who had the tremendous load of caring for a home, a husband, and two teenage children. Not only was there a sign in the front yard, there was also one in the laundry room, and one placed prominently on the kitchen cabinets. Occasionally, just to ensure the full effect and create the personal embarrassment of this teenage daughter, the slogan was carried by her mother while walking back and forth on the sidewalk in front of their home. To the total horror of this teenage girl, her mother made a point of making that march just as the school bus dropped her at the corner of their block.

As in the case of all mothers of teens, this mother was frustrated. She had picked up dirty clothes from the floor once too often. She had spanned the distance between the sink and dishwasher to relocate the dirty dishes created by her children, placing them where they should have been. That distance might as well be the grand canyon of teenage years. For some incredible reason, the forty-two-inch trek is just too much for any teen to traverse when it comes to putting away the evidence of their late-night snacks. The open food on the counter, books left scattered around the house, trash cans full to overflowing, dirty clothes left inside out when dirty or on the floor when clean—simply stated, the ingratitude of her children was more than this mother had signed on for.

So she went on strike. For one very long month she didn't clean, cook the meals, change sheets, do the laundry, or shop for groceries. There was absolutely nothing she had done previously caring for her family that she did while on strike.

The ingratitude of her children was more than this mother had signed on for.

My friend recounted that, after only two weeks, their home was disgusting. Laundry was piled high, there were no clean dishes available, and trash was overflowing. The refrigerator was bare; schoolbooks were lost in the debris. With a commitment from the father to support his wife and not touch a thing, the only clean room in the house was the parents' bedroom, and they retreated there often. These teenagers were being forced to determine if they were going to give in.

Of course, they weren't going to surrender. After all, weren't all these things part of the mom's job?

It took one more extremely long and dirty week of the family stand-off before any action was taken. The two teen children were confident their mom would give in and they would not.

I give this mom a lot of credit. Even though she hated messes, she was equally determined. She would not surrender.

By Friday evening, on the third week of this strike, my friend sneaked into the bedroom of her younger brother and they discussed the fact that they could no longer live this way. They made a plan to relent the following day and clean the house. Saying nothing to anyone else in the family, they decided they would at least lay down their arms for one day.

It took that entire Saturday, well into the evening, to get the place back into any reasonable shape. These two teenagers did work that they had previously been unexposed to. Washing every dish in the house, tackling the never-ending laundry, vacuuming, dusting, and mopping were all done that day by these two.

This very wise mother said not a word when she saw them begin the job. She simply left the house and had a day away. I know if I had been that mother, I would have walked out that door, driven away from the seeing eyes in my home, then yelled "Hurray!" in absolute unbridled elation. I'd have pulled the car over and then, to the consternation of my neighbors (who already would have thought I'd gone over the edge of insanity for putting up the sign on my front lawn in the first place), hopped out of the car and danced on the curb. In my eyes, what was taking place back at that home front would be nothing short of a miracle.

But that mom didn't end her strike that day. That mom was smart enough to realize that one cleaning day did not a change make. It was their commitment to *sharing* household duties that she wanted to achieve. She hadn't come this far for her teenagers to think that was the end of the battle. To their surprise, they were required to continue on the cleaning track, which they did. It wasn't until ten days later that she took all of her placards down. After a family meeting, with a settlement of workload shared by all members in writing, she went back to work. Her job caring for the family was still the one that accomplished the most, but for the first time her children realized what that job took.

Did that one experience mean the end of messy dishes and clothes on the floor? No. But what it created was an understanding in this family of the duties their mother performed. It also put more responsibility in the hands of each family member.

While we naturally hold the primary caretaking role on the home front, we are *mothers.* We are not *slaves.* This holds true even when we work outside of the home. It's just a natural fact; women see the things that need to be done. Our line of vision is broad in the caretaking front; we notice the things no one else does. This fact shouldn't be feared or run from. It's a good thing. Someone in the family has to first see what needs to be done and then find a way to manage this responsibility with the help of all.

We are *mothers.*
We are not *slaves.*

Your Caretaking Legacy

This strike tactic may not be one you need to instate, but the policy of sharing the home duties most assuredly is. Even if your temperament is not one so bold (this same mother also sent her physician a bill for the additional two hours she sat in the waiting room of his office before he got around to her appointment), you should take your stand. If you think you are simply placed on this earth to mop up after your family, then why are you surprised that your family thinks that of you as well?

What counts is not that so many of the household duties are "below you," it's the family's attitude when you perform those duties. At the same time you are teaching them to respect you, they will be learning a good work ethic that will serve them well all throughout life.

As Hamilton W. Mabie said, "A mother loves her child most divinely, not when she surrounds him with comfort and anticipates his wants, but when she resolutely holds him to the highest standards and is content with nothing less than his best."

What a mother actually *does* in life is so much more influential than what a mother *says.* If you speak with kind words, your daughter will. If you carefully ponder what entertainment you enjoy, your daughter will.

If you treat others and yourself with kindness and respect, you daughter will. If you develop your talents, she will develop hers.

Ultimately, when a daughter leaves to begin her own life, the decisions she makes are hers. But what you demonstrate at home helps her formulate those very decisions. It's not only the job choices or food choices you make that influence your daughter; your life and character choices will have the greatest impact.

Acting for the Best Interest of All

A story has been passed down through my family that is indeed true of my Grandmother Bunger. It was sometime in the rearing of her many children that she found herself battling for the financial care of her family. My grandfather, apparently upon receiving his check from the railroad, would stop by the local tavern on his way home after work. There the check would be cashed, drinking and gambling would finish out the evening, and he would come home after drinking too much with less than livable money in his pocket.

Grandma had children to feed and a home to maintain. This was her first priority. One day, after getting the kids off to school, this diminutive woman put on coat, hat, and gloves, then left her home. Walking first to the railroad station and into the office of the paymaster, she made her first defense for her family.

There, in no uncertain words, she told him she would be picking up her husband's check in the future. She said adamantly that she had many mouths to feed, and every red cent was needed to accomplish that task. Giving it directly to her husband would not be acceptable. She would see that the money made its way home, so she would be at his office to collect the paycheck at the end of the day, when the checks were issued. Amazingly, this man agreed to her terms.

After that, she marched to the local tavern and gave that business owner a piece of her mind. Telling him that her husband was a father with many responsibilities, she let the owner know that this establishment was not an appropriate place for her husband to spend his money. If the story runs true, Grandma Bunger's visit got Grandpa banned from the building. So he had no further opportunity to leave his family's welfare in that place.

It's interesting. My grandmother has never spoken of this story herself. Her children and her children's children are the ones who passed it on to me. Grandma Bunger always took the high road. I never heard her speak of my grandfather or treat him with anything other than utmost respect, kindness, and love. He was her husband.

Grandma Bunger always took the high road.

But neither would she allow him to make decisions that would destroy their family. Her disposition was always to hold her own, while treating everyone with grace; she would right wrongs and, at the same time, offer mercy. Perhaps because early in life she was in need of those same traits, she valued them so highly. She was masterful at combining strength of character with unconditional love.

It is not noble to let a husband destroy his family or his wife. As the wife, you are worthy of respect and gracious treatment from your husband, just as a husband should be treated in the same way by you. Verbal or physical abuse is not acceptable from a spouse—*either* spouse.

If as a mother you are accepting conduct from your husband that is destructive to you and your family, your example is flawed at best. Your daughter will be taught that compliance is necessary for peace. Yet it is never peace that is earned in such situations. What always takes place is the shrinking of one human character—the mother. Whoever a mother was meant to be, whatever she was to accomplish would be minimized under the destructive acts of their spouse.

This then would be the Home Demonstration that your daughter would see and believe these were normal relationships. No amount of words said, no counseling given could ever have the same impact as the relationship lived in front of your child.

It's not only how others treat you but how you treat others that is your legacy to your daughters. If you want your daughter to become a generous and loving woman who cares for other people, then you need to be that generous and loving woman.

No amount of words said, no counseling given could ever have the same impact as the relationship lived in front of your child.

Go on a family mission trip. Support a child in another country. Help build a house. Volunteer at the food kitchen. Pack a Shoe Box at Christmas or take an angel from the tree in the mall to buy a child's gift. Look for the big things that have impact and do them.

Yet, while those are wonderful and right things to do, are you that woman every day?

Make your daughter's friends feel welcome at your home. Love them, listen to them, hug them, and make them know how special they are. Open a door for a stranger. Let someone else get the parking spot closer to the door. Say a kind word to the harried clerk at the department store, even though you have waited in line for twenty-five very long minutes.

If we're not kind, can we expect our daughters to be? They will not be generous unless we have been. They will not seek and respond to the needs of others if we fail to respond. When a daughter sees her mother is kind, even if imperfectly so, every day of every week, she will know that is what she wants to be as well.

Wonder why your daughter may bend the rules or not tell the "exact" truth? Indeed, there is sin nature, but a more permanent influence comes from example. Integrity is becoming scarce in our society but holds so much importance. It is a fairly fundamental task to fulfill the terms of a contract, whether it's an employment agreement, a rental contract, a house purchase, or a bank loan. You don't cheat on your taxes or embezzle from your employer.

But it's just as important to never walk out of work with pens and paper that you are using for school supplies. It is imperative if given the incorrect change from a purchase, more than was due, that you immediately return it. And if you happen to make it all the way home with that change, you must drive back and turn it in. If someone drops $10 on the dressing room floor, you take it to customer service. You don't call in sick from work if you aren't sick. You don't lie, big or small.

Each and every day these things are observed by your daughter. Telling your daughter not to cheat on school work, pay what she owes, and keep her commitments when you haven't will gain you nothing but her deaf ear. Don't expect anything from her that you won't commit to yourself. Your demonstration on the home front will tell her exactly what you are willing to allow in your life as well as hers.

I've had the privilege of following in the footsteps of some of the finest women I have ever known. Ethel Anna Bunger, Alena Elizabeth Brock, Shirley Bill, and Minnie Ethel Brock are names none of you know, but they have made an indelible mark in my life—and in most everyone they encountered.

Everyone who knew them benefited by the richness of their character.

None of these women, now gone, left behind a large financial inheritance. They did not have buildings named for them, nor did they lead great institutions. But when they left this earth, they left it a better place. The wealth inherited from their lives was personal; everyone who knew them benefited by the richness of their character. It was a legacy of strength over adversity, joy with each day, commitment to truth and integrity, deeply founded faith, and unlimited love and grace for every person that entered their lives. Their character had both grit and grace. They were strong women whose history is left largely unrecorded, but their impact was made and will continue to be felt in the generations after them.

Their feats were not noble. They were ordinary kindnesses, ordinary acts, and they lived ordinary lives. But these extraordinary women were profound in their effect. They were the finest of In-Home Demonstrators.

If we know what matters most is not what we say but what we do, perhaps we will be the one leaving the footsteps that are proudly followed by the next generations. Maybe we can make it into someone's list of "People Who Have Influenced Me Most."

But most of all, we'll be leaving a life legacy that our daughters and their daughters will be blessed to follow. We will be women of grit and grace.

13

WANTED
Military Strategist

| Job Description |

Plan the conduct of warfare. Plan and strategize campaigns, the movement and disposition of forces, and the deception of the enemy.

"It's a girl!" The announcement was made in a small room—cold, sterile, unfamiliar, and filled with a group of people who were mostly strangers, people I had met all within the last twenty-four hours…well, nineteen hours to be exact. Each minute had been agonizing and relentless. But the end had arrived. The smiles behind their surgical masks showed in their eyes when the announcement came.

Next there was a loud, resounding cry. To my relief, she was healthy.

Every emotion that has ever entered my heart cascaded like Niagara Falls at that moment. Relief, love, pride, uncertainty, weariness, joy, and fear gave way to anxiousness to see and hold my baby. My husband had walked over to where they were cleaning her little body off from the process of birth. I kept asking him questions, but he is too awestruck to answer to my satisfaction.

Then, finally, they brought her to me. She was beautiful! I was amazed at the miracle. Only days before she was a kick in the rib, a blur in the ultrasound, increasing weight on the scale, and a dream. Now she was my daughter. All I could do at that moment was cry. I touched her face, her brand-new, delicate skin. Pulling her foot out from the blanket, I counted her toes. Her foot was so little, so perfect. It had an arch and toenails. As my forefinger met her hand, she wrapped her five tiny fingers around mine and looked me square in the eye. At that moment my daughter owned my heart, my life, and my best. It was hers until I died.

At that moment my daughter
owned my heart, my life,
and my best.

The Best Defense

What I didn't know that day was I had entered into a war. I had joined the ranks of the soldier defending family and home, fighting for those they love. I had not gone to the recruitment office and signed any contract. I didn't even know when I became pregnant that I would find myself in battle. This revelation came later when I discovered my child had enemies who wanted to effect change in her heart, corrupt her mind, and simply destroy her. Every child does. They had their own plan, and that plan was not for the well-being of my girl. This enemy's appearance sometimes seemed innocuous, with no obvious malicious purpose. At other times it was apparent that their intention was to inflict harm.

There are people who truly believe they are right in what they want to share with your child, in what they want to teach. Yet they are not. They can also be obvious in their destructive agenda. It is a mother who has the ability to recognize those enemies.

This child is yours and yours alone. Her family should be the one entity committed daily to her best. She has been entrusted to your care, to your protection, and needs your best defense. You as the mother are to be armed for warfare.

As in any conflict there should be Rules of Engagement—rules for battle and conduct while at war. The military describes this as "a directive issued by a competent military authority that the limitations and circumstances under which forces will initiate and prosecute combat engagements with other forces encountered." Okay, a lawyer wrote that, but what it means is that there are rules about what a soldier should do when attacked and how he or she should fight back. This instruction is given prior to shipping off.

As a mother, you're not exactly shipping off, but you are venturing into uncharted territory. This land is indeed filled with enemies and landmines. An effective Military Strategist in the form of motherhood should have her own guidelines as we march into war. These are just a few:

- You are your daughter's ally as well as her defender. She must know that you love her unconditionally and truthfully.

- Be diligent, observant, and informed of the enemies to your daughter's well-being. Guard your daughter against those who want to attack and destroy.

- Be prepared, armed, and equipped to mount an effective defense. No opportunity should be given for an enemy to gain ground in your child's mind and heart.

- Identify allies in the battle and partner with them to gain strength against hostility.

- Instruct and prepare your daughter to one day fight her own battles. It is your responsibility to make sure when you are no longer there to fight for her that she can defend herself.

- Conduct all actions on behalf of your daughter with integrity, truth, and grace. You must treat all persons with dignity and respect even if they are taking enemy positions toward your daughter.

If you are worried about the war, rest assured that we as mothers are made for battle. Fighting is not all that difficult for us moms; it comes rather easy. We have unending stamina when determined and purposed. By nature we are more tuned into people's feelings than our male counterparts, giving us the ability to catch our daughter's emotions as well as those around them. We are capable of seeing past the presentation of a person to observe the intent of a heart. Also, we possess extremely effective radar called *women's intuition*.

We are soldiers with great endurance. We outlast most around us on a daily basis; we keep battling. If nothing else, we probably could talk our enemy to death! It shouldn't be our weapon of choice, but our strength in the area of communication is a great example of our unstoppable nature.

While taking up defense for our daughters, we must be sure we understand the war we are waging and the enemy in our battle. Information about the world our daughter lives in is crucial to an effective battle plan. A clueless mother is a dangerous one. You cannot battle something you are unaware of. You must be informed. You must know what is being taught in your daughter's school, among her friends, within her culture. Without that knowledge and understanding, you won't be able to effectively defend your daughter. You'll be without the tools you need to arm yourself and then wage each battle.

A clueless mother is a dangerous one.
You cannot battle something
you are unaware of.

Don't fool yourself that your daughter is not capable of being her own worst enemy. She is. Whether it is self-image, defiant nature, or aligning herself with circumstances or friends who bring her into dangerous territory, you have to guard her even against herself. Rules are a must to keep her from entering a place in life where she is vulnerable.

Always remember, though, that while guarding against her own mistakes, she must build up her own defense weapons and armor. As I stated earlier, overprotecting is just as dangerous as underprotecting.

There are also allies, partners in this battle who will encourage you, support you, instruct you, and help both you and your daughter. As in all wars, allies are essential to win. So find those people—and fight together. They can be among her teachers, her friends, a mentor, your friends, or even in the most unusual places. Don't overlook any potential ally; he or she is priceless. They will make you and your daughter stronger for the fight.

Learning from failure

Conflicts will sometimes be won and sometimes lost. Each of the victories will be sweet; every defeat will be agonizing. But when you lose, do your best not to be discouraged. Take heart: many of the battles that are so defeating and discouraging actually bring the best results. Easy times and success don't teach the best life lessons. More often, they're learned in what is at first perceived as a failure.

Defeat instructs both you and your daughter how to get up and fight again, as well as what to do next time. Your daughter will make mistakes, and so will you. And that's fine. Learning through heartache is the best instruction available. Our goal is to avoid mistakes that alter the course of life.

As a mother, we want so badly to prevent those decisions. The ones that result in an untimely pregnancy, an alliance with peers that brings physical or emotional destruction, an auto accident with life-changing results, or a disease contracted because of a momentary lapse. There are so many life-altering possibilities for our daughters that even the thought of them can be paralyzing.

Yet know this: even if and when mistakes are made, life goes on. It's what we do with our mistakes that builds character and makes us strong. Simply never give up. Know this: grace is ahead. No matter what bad action or decision you or your daughter make in the fight, grace and mercy can be yours. Grace and mercy *will be* yours.

It is the willingness to go to war to create and act upon that military strategy that determines the successful mother in battle. Making motherhood a life priority and commitment to do your best is all that is truly needed for your daughter. Whether you spend your days on the home front or outside the home, your first role is to be a mother first. Cleaning the family bathroom or writing a legal document should never interfere with the battles you will be required to wage.

Grandma Moses

American culture has many treasures, and one of these is the legacy of Grandma Moses. The memories of this woman who lived to be 101 years old, spanning the turn of the nineteenth century, are enduring on canvas. Her artistic creations brought her fame after she was already eighty years of age. Mother of ten children, with only five who lived, a rural farmer's wife, widowed at sixty seven, Grandma Moses was a fascinating piece of the fabric of our country.

When she became a painter in her seventies because her arthritis was too bad to continue her embroidery, she portrayed in art the life that she knew. Rural pictures of American life were hung in some of the finest art galleries in the world. Her art was admired by the most powerful as well as the poorest. The simplicity in her creation as well as the simplicity in her life spoke volumes to many. And her enduring wisdom supersedes her craft. It's best stated in this quote made by her late in life.

Life is what we make it.
Always has been; always will be.
—GRANDMA MOSES

So, as mothers, why should we work so hard in this unrelenting battle? Why should we look for the enemies and create a strategy? Because the result is ultimately important. You are helping to shape a human life—your daughter's. It is not the book we write, the car we help manufacture, the store we run, the letter we type, nor the house we clean that will truly affect the generations that follow. It is the daughters we bring into this world and help to mold. They are our treasures, and they will be this world's treasure as well. Your parenting has a profound effect on your daughter's life.

In the simple lyrics of John Mayer, the family life and love cycle is profoundly portrayed. "So fathers, be good to your daughters, daughters will love like you do. Girls become Lovers who turn into mothers, so Mothers be good to your daughters too."

There is no more profound joy in life but to see your daughter become what she is destined to be—with the strength, grace, and courage to face her own future, fulfill her own destiny, and follow her dreams. It is worth the cost, the commitment, the fight.

Military Strategist, plan and execute well. Then our homes both now and down the road will have lasting peace. And through our daughters we raise, our nation will be a better place for all.

Conclusion

<u>Wanted</u>

Take the Job!

| Job Description |

Seeking women willing to take the most difficult job in the world—raising daughters. No experience necessary.

What began as an auto accident and a trip to the doctor turned into one of the most rewarding, frustrating, challenging, delightful, and agonizing of jobs. Yet this has been the job that has impacted my life the most. It has not only shaped the lives of my daughters but mine as well. I have gained strength, grace, resilience, patience, been given mercy, and learned how to give mercy. It has made me richer than any other endeavor I have undertaken.

My two daughters are the treasure of my life, and I have no regrets...not because I did everything right, but because I wholeheartedly committed to undertake this life calling to the best of my abilities.

To be a good mother, you simply have to accept the job. Not just the birth of a baby, the purchase of a cradle, or the changing of the diapers, but the job itself. So say yes. *Take this job!*

Countless women have had children while never making a conscious decision that this would indeed be their life occupation.

Instead, predetermine that you will be one when challenged to stand up. As long days turn into late nights, you stay on call. You mend injuries, dry tears, encourage and protect, staying attune to the needs of your child. You are the one to expect their very best. The rules are yours to set, which you do, and to enforce, which you will. The range of emotion will plunge from delight to heartbreak and back to joy again, yet you will stay on course, determined to complete this task. So Mom, accept this job.

There is no more important or fulfilling life career than being a mother. I can confidently assure you the rewards will forever be worth any amount of pain. You may have your own President or maybe you are raising the mother of a President. Whatever your daughter's destiny you can help make it happen!

There is no more important or fulfilling life career than being a mother.

Several years ago, our family went on a month-long adventure, an extensive vacation out west. Los Angeles, the Grand Canyon, the Mohave Desert, Big Bear, and many other sites were included in this trip. Halfway through our travels we met up with some very dear friends of ours who, like us, have two daughters.

Their elder daughter, indeed their explorer, was celebrating a special birthday and wanted to see Las Vegas. This was the short era in which Las Vegas was promoting family vacations and it appealed to her. She researched the pools at the hotels, the architecture of the buildings, the restaurants, and a million other interesting things Las Vegas offered. It wasn't a city you would expect to have family fun in but they, like our family, have a firm belief that when you have a child who is destined to see the world, you want that child to see a lot of it with you at their side (of course, all the while providing your commentary, attitudes, and perspectives throughout the trip while having fun). So this was the plan.

We did have three days of fun, saw some great buildings, went to Imax movies, shopped at the M&M store, went to an art gallery, and so much more. But there is no question that this city exists for what it is known: self-indulgence in every way.

As our two families were walking down the street, we happened upon flyers promoting a strip club. These had been stuck in the railing of one of the walking bridges for all to see. My daughter, picking up the photograph of a very attractive yet partially clothed young woman, decided she would remedy the situation. She gathered up each one she saw and immediately placed them in the nearest trash can. Always headstrong, she was determined to make a difference.

When I told her they would just be back and put more out, she asked me why. Not why would they be back, or why were the flyers put there in the first place. She was astute enough to figure out why men would want to go to these clubs and what it would take to get them there. But she wanted to know: why would the woman in the photo allow herself to work there, demoralized, at that sex club? Didn't she think more of herself than that?

I struggled to explain that often life difficulties encourage women to make decisions that don't seem logical. We don't live their lives or have their struggles, but somewhere along the line they decide this is the road for them. I completed my explanation with saying that we don't have to agree with their choices, but we are to love anyone who makes life choices that we see as destructive. We can feel sad, extend understanding, and pray for them. We can offer love and support anytime we have the opportunity.

Everything I said was true. But as I listened to myself, it sounded like a list of platitudes, the patronizing dialect of a disconnected mother.

As we walked on, all I could think of for the rest of the day was *She is somebody's little girl.* That young lady on that flyer was someone's baby wrapped in the hospital blanket and handed to her mother. She wore pink bows, lost her front teeth in kindergarten, brought home a report card, had a first kiss, and left her family to follow a dream. She was once just a little girl. Perhaps her family wasn't secure enough or strong enough to nurture her. Of maybe she didn't have anyone to guide her and help her in life.

She is somebody's little girl.

Each step walking through this city brought me nearer to the reality that this young woman was not always "the woman who worked at the strip club." She, like every other grown woman in our nation, began life as a precious, hopeful, trusting baby girl. That day a place was seared in my heart that screamed, *There have to be more women willing to take this job, the job that provides direction and gives hope!*

There is such a need to guide the sweet little jump-rope skipper on the elementary school playground to becoming a self-confident, fulfilled woman. But each little girl only has this chance if every mother is willing to take this job. If the mother chooses not to, that little girl will follow the paths that break our hearts.

Indeed, children do not come with a job description or an employee training manual. In fact, you don't even receive that little booklet that comes with the power drill or curling iron. Your initial encounter with the firstborn arrives when you are truly clueless without a "this is your daughter and what she requires" instruction manual. But this is your baby girl. You can't go home and leave that daughter behind. It's your home, and she lives there.

The mothering job is not found by reading the paper or through a job search program. It doesn't require you to apply for it, face an interview, or have your qualifications reviewed. You don't have to be extended an offer to reject or accept and work under someone else's direction.

Motherhood begins by having a baby. You become pregnant and birth a baby, or you adopt a baby. You may even find you become a mother through marriage. Whichever way this job begins, now you're a mother. If you are the least bit sane, your daughter should arrive with a mixture of emotions. At the moment you see her precious face you are filled with unrelenting love, hope, delight, awe, and relief. It doesn't take long to add the emotions of terror, self-doubt, confusion, even despair. If those feelings arrive, you are indeed a sane and sensible woman and truly qualified for this position. This is the real deal—you truly hold the responsibility for another human.

When you tire and want to slack up on being the authority (and you will), remember this is your job. The shaping of human character is created by your actions and your daughter's success will depend upon you.

As fearful as this may seem there are some great moments that make this all worthwhile. These will be special memories in ordinary days to remind you what a joy this job really is.

When you:

- Hold your two-year-old, and she twirls your hair along with hers, whispering, "I love you, Mommy."
- Arrive at the elementary school and, upon entering your daughter's classroom, she leaps from her desk, runs across the room, and throws her arms around your legs.
- Have a cackle of "middle-school" girls underfoot in the kitchen as you are trying to find something for the clan to eat, and they are regaling every minute detail of their overly dramatic lives.
- Become the one mother the high school group is okay with attending the extra-curricular event, even though they know you enforce the rules.
- Are asked to be the special person to help decorate your daughter's dorm room as she leaves home for her first real "independent" venture into life.

- Pick up the phone at all hours, day and night. because you are the one she calls with grown-up questions about grown-up life.

Then you know taking the job was worth all you gave—including the tears, the frustration, and the sheer delights.

The effect of successful mothers has been lauded for centuries and is better said by others than myself:

Let France have good mothers, and she will have good sons.
—NAPOLEON BONAPARTE

For the mother is and must be, whether she know it or not, the greatest, strongest and most lasting teacher her children have.
—HANNAH W. SMITH

Who is it that loves me and will love me forever with an affection which no chance, no misery, no crime of mine can do away? It is you, my mother.
—THOMAS CARLYLE

One of the oldest human needs is having someone to wonder where you are when you don't come home at night.
—MARGARET MEAD

The mother is the most precious possession of the nation, so precious that society advances its highest well-being when it protects the functions of the mother.
—ELLEN KEY

All that I am and hope to be I owe to my angel mother.
—ABRAHAM LINCOLN

These statements and many more like them are never said about anyone other than a mom. Accolades made from the platform of an awards presentation or simply a family at the dining room table declares the worth of a good mother. The impact this position can make is undisputed.

So now you know. At least you know a lot of the jobs that need to be done. It may look a lot more like work to you than when you found out you were going to be a mom or even when you began this book. But don't let that scare you. Every one of our daughters desperately *need* for you to take this job.

So Mom, take the job. You can do this; it is not an impossible task. In fact, the rewards are great. You'll be building an amazing relationship with an amazing girl...*your girl.* Together you and she will learn, grow, achieve, and conquer things you never thought possible.

Know that your girl will have the opportunity to excel in life—to become everything she is created to be. Just because you, her mom, make the commitment to take and complete the most difficult job in the world: raising daughters.

Founded by Darlene and Dan R. Brock in 2011, The Grit and Grace Project is a company dedicated to helping **Women** reach their full potential, merging two of the primary strengths innate to women, **Grit** and **Grace**, calling upon those strengths to find purpose as **Individuals, Wives**, and **Mothers.**

| GRIT |

Firmness of character; indomitable spirit, toughness and resolution; unyielding courage in the face of hardship or danger

| GRACE |

Freely given unmerited favor and mercy; moral strength;
a disposition of generosity and kindness;
favor rendered even when you need not do so

The Grit and Grace Project

P. O. Box 247
Estero, FL 33929
239-349-2600
info@thegritandgraceproject.com

www.thegritandgraceproject.com
www.oaktara.com

About the Author

DARLENE BROCK grew up in a small Indiana town known primarily for the automobiles it produced in the '20s and '30s—the Auburn, Cord, and Duesenberg. Desiring more freedom and adventure than a small town afforded, she left home two weeks after her high school graduation and began her foray into the workplace.

Holding a short-term office job at a local church, Darlene quickly discovered at the age of eighteen that perhaps she wasn't "church" material. She was then hired at a very political and influential law firm as a receptionist. This big Indiana city law office exposed her to the world of politics and provided her with a raw, in-depth perspective into the legal profession. This experience ultimately piloted Darlene toward a growing conviction that she needed more purpose in her life. Although she wasn't at the time "church" material, she desired something more than the "success" she observed that was attained through power, wealth, and influence.

It was then she left the political and legal world behind, moving to live and work in a Christian commune located in northern Ohio. She headed a girl's home, which was part of a community social service initiative that took in indigents and runaways. The girls in the home ran a cleaning company, grew their own food, and participated in intense Bible studies. Leaving a highly political office environment to join the young communal mindset of the time, Darlene discovered the fulfillment and purpose she desired, yet rejected the narrow and legalistic side of that lifestyle.

Upon that realization she returned to Indiana to oversee a retreat center and summer campground. It was there during a Music Industry Retreat Darlene met her future husband, Dan R. Brock, who was in attendance. Later on a road trip with a friend to Nashville, she met up again with Dan. It was then he offered Darlene her first job in the music industry. Accepting the position, she then relocated to Music City, Nashville, Tennessee.

Diligence, hard work, and a self-starter mindset led Darlene to become the third most successful agent (after Dan and his partner) at the TAME Agency, which represented a large number of prominent acts. In 1978, Dan and Darlene married and moved to Oklahoma City. There they founded Brock & Associates, their own personal management and booking agency representing early Christian rockers Petra and DeGarmo & Key.

The genre of Contemporary Christian Music was in its infancy, and the Brocks were pioneers in a new frontier. Expanding their business led to the formation of Creative Concerts, the concert promotion arm of B&A. Darlene led this venture, traveling and producing concerts throughout the U.S., learning how to adapt and build relationships with a diverse array of individuals in equally diverse cities. It was in Oklahoma, during that busy time, that both of her daughters were born.

The Brocks moved back to Nashville in 1987 and continued to manage several acts through their company.

In 1988 ForeFront Records was launched in the kitchen of their Music Row management office. Dan began the label with partners DeGarmo & Key and producer Ron W. Griffin. Darlene immediately served various capacities within this young company while continuing her role as co-manager to Brock & Associates' artists.

In 1990, when Dan became President and CEO of ForeFront, Darlene began her solo flight in personal management with DC

Talk and Geoff Moore & the Distance. Success in that role included multiple Grammy and Dove nominations and awards for her management clients, as well as awards for videos produced by Darlene. At the same time she served as COO of ForeFront, overseeing employees and business interests at this growing multimillion-dollar record and music publishing group.

Darlene's daughters grew up while she worked full-time in her various business roles. They were exposed to all aspects of the music industry, from traveling to concerts with her, attending awards programs, to rollerblading outside of the edit bay when she was producing music videos.

In 1996 ForeFront was acquired by EMI from Dan and current co-owner Eddie DeGarmo. The Brocks retired from the music business in 1999, then relocated to Florida in 2001.

In 2011, after an extended semi-retired phase, Darlene announced the formation of The Grit and Grace Project—an organization dedicated to helping Women reach their full potential and find purpose as Individuals, Wives, and Mothers.

Help Wanted: Moms Raising Daughters is the Company's first release.

To write Darlene: **info@thegritandgraceproject.com**

www.thegritandgraceproject.com
www.oaktara.com